Siranus Sver

QUANTUM ENERGY

The Secret of Extraordinary Change and Healing

How to use more than sixty exercises that can radically change your life!

Copyright © 2024 Siranus Sven Von Staden
All rights reserved
First Edition

PAGE PUBLISHING
Conneaut Lake, PA

First originally published by Page Publishing 2024

Exercises and information in this book are not a substitute for medical or therapeutic treatment.

ISBN 979-8-88793-243-9 (pbk)
ISBN 979-8-88793-250-7 (digital)

Printed in the United States of America
Translation by Rita LaRue

DISCLAIMER OF LIABILITY

The author and publisher shall have neither liability nor responsibility to any person or entity with respect to any loss or damage caused or alleged to be caused directly or indirectly by the information contained in this book. While the book is as accurate as the author can make it, there may be errors, omissions, and inaccuracies.

Readers take responsibility for any consequences incurred in performance of the exercises contained in this book. Neither the author nor the publisher is liable for any consequences resulting in the practical instructions given in this book.

This book contains references to websites whose contents are not subject to the author nor the publisher's liability. No guarantee is given for this content.

All rights of distribution, including by radio, television, and other means of communication, photomechanical or set reproduction as well as the reprint are reserved in extracts.

First originally published by Page Publishing 2024

All rights reserved. No part of this book may be reproduced, by any means, without written permission of the author or publisher, except by a reviewer quoting brief excerpts for a review in a magazine, newspaper, website, or radio.

CONTENTS

Foreword xi
Introduction to the Extended Version xiii
Preface xvii

Part 1: The Method of Quantum Energy 1
   How It All Started 3
   A Brief Overview Of The New Transformation Methods 7
   The Big Difference To Traditional Healing And
      Therapy Methods 9
   What Exactly Is "Quantum Energy"? 13
   Why Is "Quantum Energy" So Special? 20
   Your Prerequisites For Success 31
   The Kinesiological Test 36
   The Four Areas Of Life 37

Part 2: Quantum Energy and Health 39
   Health And Healing 41
   How You Can Feel The Energy That Leads To
      Change And Healing 43
   Your Body As Perfect Signal Giver 45
   Faith And Health: A Life's Model 47
   Transform Profound Mental Beliefs And Patterns
      Relating To Healing 58
   Get Rid Of Fears, Phobias, And Panic Attacks 69
   Activate Your Self-Healing Powers 75
   Stress And Burnout 78
   Get Rid Of Allergies 88
   Heal Physical Pain 89

How To Heal Injuries 96
Alzheimer's And Dementia 98

Part 3: Quantum Energy and Relationships 105
Relationships And Healing 106
Your Relationship With Yourself 108
Your Deepest Need 112
Pain Or Joy? 119
Your Worst Traumas 122
Transform Your Behavioral Patterns In Relation To Love 124
The Relationship With Your Partner 130
The Role Of The Partner In Your Theater Of Life 131
Get Rid Of Fears And Beliefs 141
Looking For Your Dream Partner 142
The Relationship With Your Parents 147
The Relationship With Your Children 157
From The Alleged Disease ADHD 162
Relationships With Your Friends, Colleagues, And Neighbors ...167
Letting Go Made Easier When Releasing Ties 168

Part 4: Quantum Energy and Success/Wealth 175
Success And Healing 177
The Myth Of Success 178
A New Philosophy On Success 180
From Lack Consciousness To Abundance Consciousness 182
The Lack Caused During Two World Wars 185
Your Focus Determines Your Success In Life 187
Be The Creator 190
The Physio-Magic 193
The Why In Your Life 198
Your Big Threes 205
Define Your Goals 210
Activate Potentials That Are Necessary For Achieving
    Your Vision And Goals 215
A Clear Direction 220
The Clear Focus 223

    Strengthening Strengths—The Path To Your Calling............225
    Transform Your Blockages In Regard To Success...................227
    Transform Profound Behavioral Patterns In Relation
        To Your Success 234
    Experience Wealth On All Levels..235

Part 5: Quantum Energy and Spirituality 245
    Spirituality And Healing 247
    The Question And Meaning Of Your Life 249
    Recognize Your Individual Spirituality.....................................253
    Become Free Of Ratings, Judgments, And Guilt......................256
    The Ease Of "I Am!" 259
    Experience Yourself In Source Consciousness 262
    Gratitude..263
    Activate Unused Spiritual Potential 267
    Realize Your Own Mastery 270
    Experience The Essence...272
    Experience The Universal Impulses 276
    Experience The Soul And Body As A Unit 280
    Experience Everyday Life Completely New With The
        Help Of Source Consciousness...285
    Quantum Energy And Distant Healing....................................287

Closing Word..290
Testimonials on Working with "Quantum Energy"......................292
Perception Redefined 294
Closing Words (with Gratitude) 296
Directory...298

With love and gratitude for my beautiful wife Sonja Ariel Von Staden.

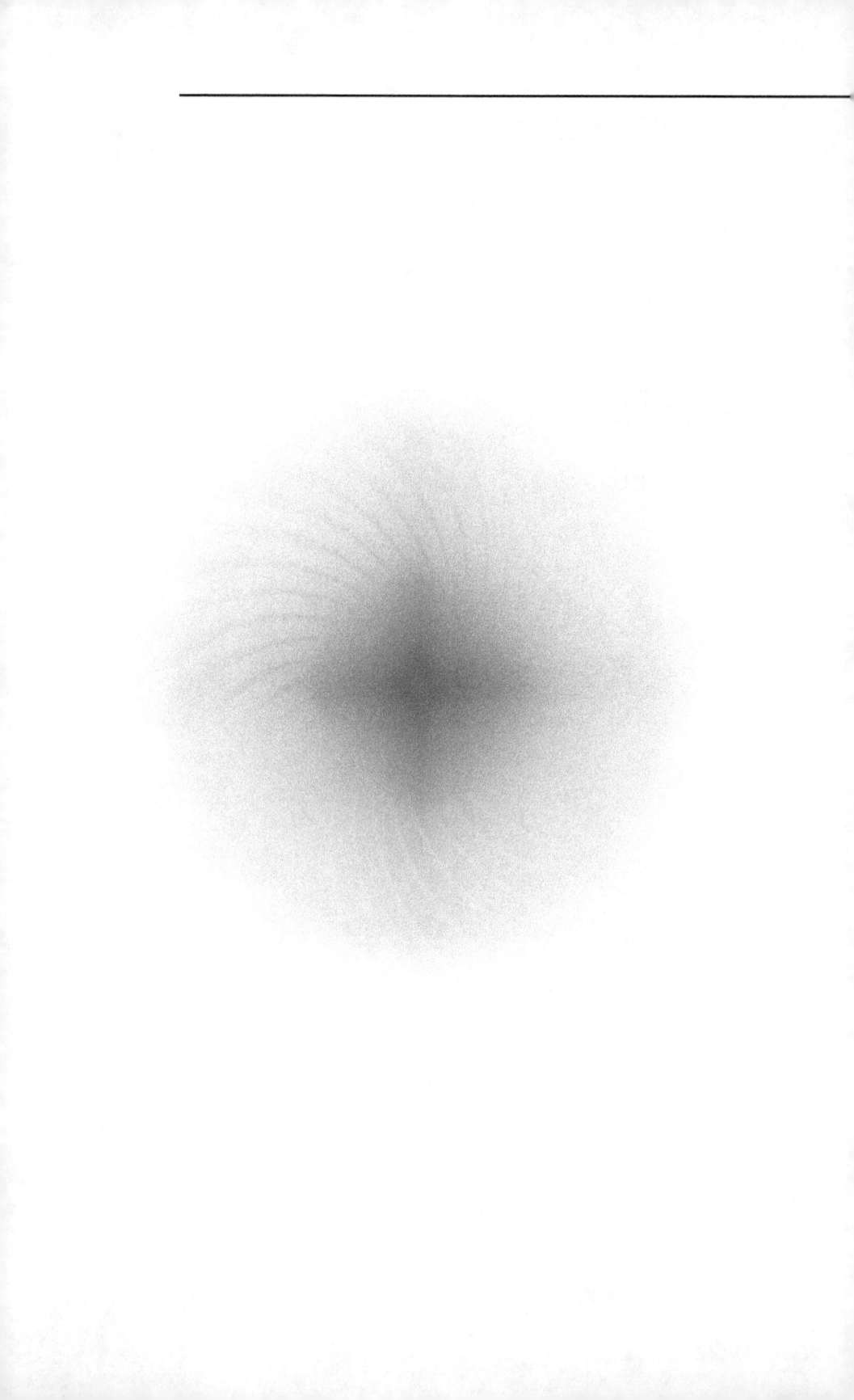

FOREWORD

"Self-experience" and "self-healing" as well as the "development of individual consciousness" are topics which, today, more and more people are interested in. In the past, access to this was through ideological concepts, with providers of spiritual transformation methods using an esoteric language that is widely used in sections of the population, however, was not well received. Now this situation is beginning to change due to advances in basic scientific research. In particular, the findings of quantum physics and biophysics provide a new linguistic foundation, which refers to concrete physical terms and their interactions. We now know that human consciousness and the control of biological metabolic processes described by quantum fields can be used. Feelings and thoughts can also be expressed through chemical milieus in our cells and through electromagnetic fields. The concentration and distribution of biophotons in our body is decisive for the vitality and state of consciousness and for our emotional and mental condition.

In his book, Siranus Sven von Staden succeeds in quantum and biophysics and applies it to the spiritual transformation of humans. It describes a series of effective exercises and methods by which individuals become aware of their individual self-healing potential and shows how this can be applied to the respective life situation.

"Quantum energy" can be used positively in all areas of your daily life. All for the management of health problems, the reduction of stress, the resolution of relationship conflicts in partnerships, family, and social environment, as well as for the positive unfolding of

FOREWORD

one's own gifts and creativity. "Quantum energy" is an effective way to achieve a higher quality of life.

Dr. Michael König
Quantum Physicist and Author
(known from the movie (R)Evolution 2012)

INTRODUCTION TO THE EXTENDED VERSION

I thought long about how to deal with all the knowledge and experience of "quantum energy." This matter is close to my heart, and I wanted to share this information with the world. I asked myself first if I should write a second book of "quantum energy" as so many other authors have done. The idea would have been financially attractive, but I decided not to, despite marketing principles. So now, you are holding the extended edition of my first work *Quantum Energy* in your hands.

Is an extended version necessary? you ask yourself. The answer is a clear yes. Since the book was finished, an infinite amount has happened. I conducted hundreds of coaching sessions using these methods, a lot of seminars, and already completed seven annual trainings, as well as quantum energy coaching in various locations in Germany, Switzerland, and Ibiza, Spain. During this time, I was able to gain experience that had not yet been incorporated into the first edition. Now you will learn and benefit from all these experiences and improvements.

I was firmly convinced that the book *Quantum Energy* would be a success, but that success would come so quickly, I really did not expect it at all. The first edition of the book was sold out only after a few weeks. Five weeks after that, it was already a bestseller for Schirner Publisher (Germany). Within one year, I was one of the most successful authors for Schirner. The subsequent books written after that also became Schirmer's bestsellers. *Quantum Energy* appeared within less than one year in the fourth edition. I really don't want to

INTRODUCTION

sound like I am bragging; I am only telling you this to show you how much the new healing methods are needed and absorbed by everyone in the truest sense of the word. It also shows you what it does when you follow your gift and act in clarity. Because that is what I did. With *Quantum Energy*, I have made my biggest contribution to the world, and that is why you are holding the extended edition in your hands. I feel it is my duty to share with you my new insights. I have made changes, improvements, and simplifications consciously, brought in user testimonials on specific topics in order to make the book livelier for you and to encourage you, above all, to apply "quantum energy" immediately. Tens of thousands are already using the method successfully.

Furthermore, I have complied reader requests and have expanded all five parts of the book by adding new topics and more exercises for you. The previous fifty-five exercises have now turned into sixty-three. Now the book can be beneficial to both—those who are beginning to understand the new healing methods and those who have already read one of the first four editions. To anticipate any questions, the exercise CDs still contain the new exercises, and the practice CDs still do not contain the new exercises. However, they are to be extended with the next edition.

It is an honor, and I am pleased that you have chosen this book and have decided to have a more fulfilling life.

I wish you every success, fun, and love with *Quantum Energy*.

Sinaw Sue v. Stack

Ibiza, October 2012

With Rita LaRue, English Translation and Literature Agent, Dallas, Texas 2023

PREFACE

We live in a wonderful and exciting time. Provided that we like change. Rarely did the changes feel so drastically as they do today, and rarely before have they moved so much, be it September 11, 2001, the tsunami disaster at the end of 2004, or the myth of our end around December 21, 2012. Nothing remains the same. The Internet, although developed more than thirty years ago, is—as Michael Dell used to say years ago—about the same as the Ford Model T: "It works and is revolutionary for this time, but it will develop dramatically over the next ten years, like the cars since the Ford Model T." Here is how it is: the World Wide Web is almost limitless and enables things that we still would not even have dared to dream. And despite this age, it is still in its infancy.

Much has also happened in the scientific sector. The new sciences, as they are called, highlight aspects and statements by Newton and Descartes. (The quantum physics, developmental or cell biology, always new revolutionary discoveries). The world of possibilities is growing, whether we want to believe it or not. It is almost like when people thought that the world was flat; at some point, there was someone who went on a long journey to find out that there was no end, and he kept going with his ship. In one moment, the faith of humanity changed. We seem to be at a similar point at this moment.

In current times, it is not surprising that the promise of healing at all levels became popular. Ten years ago, it was still reserved for a few healers to achieve spectacular health. The founders of the new procedures promised that there would be self-healing and changes at all levels possible by every human. In Russia, methods have already been sufficiently developed to allow organs and teeth to be regrown.

PREFACE

People have also become aware of the new methods that can already cure cancer or AIDS. Success and wealth can also be positively influenced.

I am a person who believes in the unusual. The statement of profound self-healing was, even for me, too bold and awakened my inner critic. Should it indeed be possible for everyone, without any prior experience, to be able to bring profound changes and healing to themselves and other people? I became curious and tried it out for myself according to the motto: "Try it, otherwise you will never know."

Today I can say, yes, it is true! Anyone can learn and apply these new methods. They are revolutionary psychology and medicine in equal measure. The wisdoms of quantum consciousness, such as I would like to call them, are millennia-old and new knowledge at the same time. They combine ancient spiritual wisdom with the latest scientific knowledge.

The method "quantum energy" described here was taken from the wisdoms of quantum consciousness. In addition to the new findings, I also included the most successful exercises in my experience of some conventional methods. These exercises have three prerequisites: they are fast, easy, and successful to apply. You will learn about them in this book. But do not just read about spectacular healings or changes that quantum energy enables. This book is a workbook. These readings convey knowledge, but the emphasis is on its practical application. Therefore, the theory is secondary. If you need more background knowledge, you will find this in the back of the book and furthermore in movie recommendations. This book will guide you directly into "quantum energy"—with more than sixty exercises and many more suggestions. You can start and apply these exercises immediately and successfully change and heal areas in your life, be it for your health, your relationships, your success, or your spirituality.

HOW YOU CAN APPLY THIS BOOK

You can read this book like any other book and work and choose any areas of your life that you would like to change or improve. You can also use it as a work reference if you only want to tackle a specific topic, like disease, pain, or wealth. Simply search in the table of contents, or practice according to the corresponding topic. Many exercises can be done directly. For others, however, I recommend the practice CD set for this book. Some meditations are simple to carry out but so complex that you will probably not be able to imitate them by heart.

This could influence the success of the exercises. Note that even for the less complex exercises, it always applies: first read the exercise completely, then perform it.

It is also important to test in advance every exercise whether the time is right for the change. Because it is not always the right moment. I noticed this many times with my clients. To test it, I recommend the "kinesiological" test (see page 36).

Certainly, you can also use the exercises for others. To do this, simply instruct the individual as you learned the exercises. Remote healing is also possible. More about that at the end of the book.

As "wisdom of quantum consciousness," I describe it as the totality of spiritual and scientific knowledge. The various findings are integrated into the texts and exercises of this book but not listed individually. Obviously, the book can represent only a part of it.

I have a vision of helping millions of people live a carefree, healthier, happier, and fulfilling life. We live in a time when this is easily possible—whether you believe or not. So take advantage of the insights and wisdom of this era. *Quantum Energy* is my contribution

PREFACE

to the world. As more people read this book, the more they get to know the methods and apply them, the sooner my vision will become a reality.

Someone told me that my final word should be the foreword. For me, it is perfect as it is. It may be important for you to read the final words at the beginning. Then I invite you to do so now.

I wish you lots of pleasure in reading and performing the various exercises. If you have any questions about different areas, or to individual exercises, to coaching, to workshops, or to train as a quantum energy coach, just contact me anytime.

From my heart,
Siranus Sven von Staden
Leverkusen, Germany, September 2010

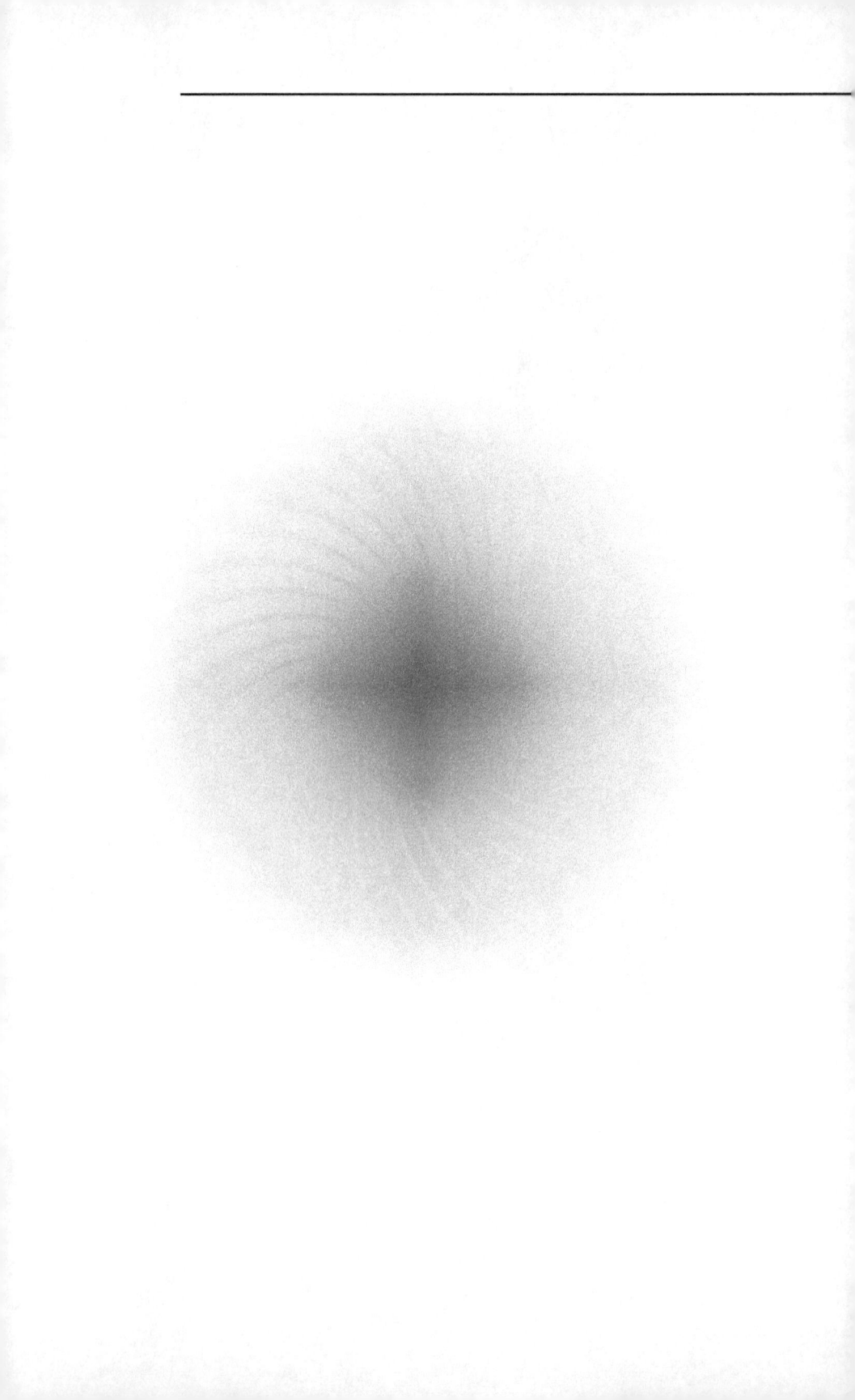

PART I

The Method of Quantum Energy

THE METHOD OF QUANTUM ENERGY

HOW IT ALL STARTED

> "Every beginning is something special—
> possibly the beginning of a great love."
> —Siranus Sven Von Staden

It all started in the beginning of July 2009. My wife, Sonja, and I were invited to dinner with friends. We had a lot of fun and enjoyed the food very much. After the meal, our friends told us about a seminar they had attended a few weeks earlier. The seminar topic was "Career and Finances, a "Path to the Extraordinary." However, this should not be done using traditional methods. A so-called two-point method would make it possible to identify behavioral patterns that affect the flow of energy for career and money in the way of spontaneously changing the flow so the flow could run freely.

At that moment, my mind was overwhelmed. One side of me said, "That's cool!" while the other side immediately awakened my inner critic. They (both in the coaching business) shared that since the seminar was over, they had increased business within a short time and with a volume that they never had experienced before. Making €12,000 (approximately $15,000) was a very convincing argument. I quickly settled my inner critic.

I was curious. I wanted to know more. At this point, I worked as a coach and coached for many years. I worked with individuals or companies on the topic of "change." I knew all too well how long it could take for profound changes to take place. Should there be a method which would make the time factor almost irrelevant? Almost unbelievable, but I was intrigued. If there is something new that will change and expedite the process to the benefit of my clients, I wanted to know more.

So I sat down at my laptop and researched the Internet for the topic "two-point method." I came across the method "Matrix Energetics 2," a concept developed by Dr. Richard Bartlett in the USA. In addition, I also found the date for the next seminar in Germany, which was already fully booked. Well, there seemed to be something about the subject. I signed up for the next seminar date in August 2009. I wanted to educate myself about this legendary method.

I admit, I was a little excited, which normally does not happen easily. Together with seventy other participants, I experienced two breathtaking days with many unusual moments. I learned that the two-point method is not a cure in the conventional sense and that it works at the quantum level. What that means, you will find in the next subpart.

With this new knowledge and experience, I came home. Of course, I had to share this with my wife and went straight to practice—and it worked. I was super excited to be able to share this new information at my upcoming weekend workshop. I informed my participants that I would like to share this revolutionary method, and that whoever wanted to experience and practice this method on themselves, they could. I offered two half-day workshops. Four participants came to the morning class, nine in the afternoon. Two spectacular changes that day left all doubts evaporated: one participant's nerve pathways that had been injured a few years ago by a fracture of the cervical spine were reactivated—although we were working on a completely different topic! In another participant, her perception widened so much and to the extent that she was suddenly able to see the aura[1] of other individuals.

My curiosity was awakened. After that experience, I started to research everything that had to do with these new healing meth-

---

[1] The aura or energy body of a person is a radiation, which, for mentally or otherwise sensitive people, is a color spectrum that surrounds the body in a cloud or light wreath.

ods. For example, "quantum healing" by Dr. Frank Kinslow and *Reconnective Healing* by Dr. Eric Pearl. In addition, I absorbed everything on this subject that had to do with the scientific background of it.

The New Science[2] offered a great deal of information on this. I went and visited the founders of these methods, tried them all, and was extremely surprised by the results. I found out that, as different as some of these methods were, they all worked on the same basis. Back then, Richard Bandler and John Grinder must have also found, as they analyzed the best therapists at the time, what made it possible for them to achieve such success. The fact was that all the basic strategies were the same. Bandler and Grinder used these extraordinary strategies, gathered all the relevant information, and the result was neuro-linguistic programming (NLP)[3], a method that is not only used worldwide today in therapists and neuropathologist applications but also very successfully used in our economy. I was so fascinated when I discovered this method and had Richard Bandler train me personally. This new knowledge enhanced my work as a trainer and coach tremendously.

Back to the new healing methods. It was clear to me that I had to incorporate the new knowledge into my seminars and coachings from now on. This should only the beginning. After long research and applying these new methods, I felt that this work was something that would change my own life. I had set myself up to the task and path to help people find "true greatness." From NLP, I knew some techniques that would allow me to achieve change quickly. With these new healing methods, it was suddenly feasible to bridge

---

[2] The New Sciences are those that have separated themselves from traditional sciences and represent an expanded worldview. These include quantum physics, epigenetics, or morphogenetics. It shows today in scientific experiments, what the Indigenous peoples already knew in the millennia. New scientists include Gregg Braden, Bruce Lipton, Dieter Broers, Michael König, John Hagelin, William Tiller, and Rupert Sheldrake.

[3] Neurolinguistic programming (NLP) was developed in the 1970s. It is, in my opinion, one of the most successful methods of communication, motivation, and changes.

time and space and to bring changes and healings immediately. The individuals that already had experienced quantum energy could suddenly feel the difference to other healing methods. This was the icing on the cake of my previous work and should be, from now on, a huge part of my life.[4] Typically, I do not execute other folks' concepts; I want my own. However, there should be no further method needed because there were already enough. I decided it should be something that unites the new methods—their essence and all my knowledge and experience from many years of NLP, energy, and personality work.

The result was "quantum energy," a method that is scientifically proven where exceptional changes and healings happen—fast, easy, highly effective, and sustainable. Those who experience quantum energy feel the difference to other new healing methods.

---

[4] After only three years, I achieved the greatest earning potential that I ever had in training and coaching.

A BRIEF OVERVIEW OF THE NEW TRANSFORMATION METHODS

"Everything is energy. Consciously used, it creates reality."

For the past years, people's consciousness has been changing in Germany and in other Western countries. It feels like we are living in a revolution of consciousness. It reflects in the reports in renowned magazines and television documentaries, which are increasingly broadcasting similar subjects. More often, you will find on major magazine's cover pages' topics on the question of the meaning of life, alternative healing methods, and such.

Let us look at the new healing methods. They mostly come from the USA and were often developed or founded by doctors. Examples are the authors mentioned above—Dr. Richard Bartlett, Dr. Frank Kinslow, and Dr. Eric Pearl. All three are originally chiropractors who made an astonishing discovery at some point: they were able to heal their clients without performing a special chiropractic application. As they practiced this new way of healing, the more positive results they had.

From Russia comes a healing method which is called the New Healing Methods from Russia.[5] It was founded by Grigori Grabovoi, Dr. Arkadij Petrov, Igor Aprepjew, Nadezhda and Vladim Korolev. According to them, the healing successes makes it possible to regrow organs and teeth.

---

[5] See the video on the Arkadij Petrov Foundation's website: http://petrovfond.de/film.html. The German version is available at http://mediathek.viciente.at/der-ewige-jungbrunnen-russen-lassen-organe-und-zaehne-nachwachsen.

THE METHOD OF QUANTUM ENERGY

These are the most well-known facts known to me. There may be more, but this is just an example of what is possible now.

As different as these methods may be, they all work and follow a remarkably similar principle: they use a form of energy that we generally cannot see. We can only feel it. It is an energy available to us twenty-four hours a day. The energy from which all substance exists in our universe.

Quantum physics also states that everything in the universe is energy. All things like a chair, a table, or a toothbrush are made of the same "substance" as water, gases, or the air we breathe. The only difference is that the energy is more compacted when the substance is hard. Probably the largest compaction and the hardest material we know is the diamond. The air has extraordinarily little compaction. Our consciousness, our thoughts, and our feelings represent a very subtle form of energy, but how strong this force can be, we all notice when we are really in love, sad, or angry. Everything is energy, which is constantly in motion, in vibration. Even the energy of a mountain or a reinforced concrete building is in motion, but we cannot see it.

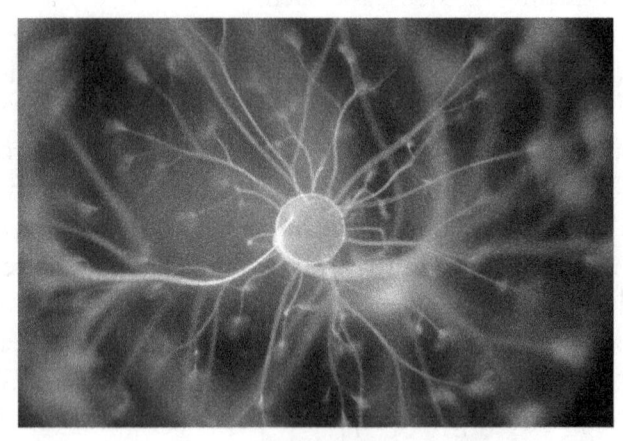

All is energy

Methods such as "Matrix Energetics," quantum healing, "reconnective healing," or the Russian healing methods use exactly this energy as well as one's own creativeness for healing. In many ways, so does "quantum energy."

THE BIG DIFFERENCE TO TRADITIONAL HEALING AND THERAPY METHODS

> "Everything is connected to everything," say scientists;
> let us use this wisdom and create miracles!

Healing and its methods are probably as old as humanity itself. There always have been healers, whether they were a medicine man, a shaman, or healing priests. Probably the biggest difference was that these skills were passed down to other generations and made it possible for only a few to be able to heal others. Most likely, they had to learn incredibly unique techniques. Gods had to be worshipped, ghosts summoned, certain earthly cycles had to pass, special sequences be observed, angels were involved, etc. In most cases, you were not able to heal until you had become a master or had been appointed to a master healer.

I would like to use all these examples as the "old tradition" or the "old energy." The word "old" is meant without evaluation in the sense of "other." All these methods had their place, and that is a good thing. They are likely to continue to be used, which is also good and important for many people.

Over the past years, we have seen an increase in earth's energy. We may have noticed this because time somehow seems to pass faster. Learning is also faster. Ten years ago, we had four days to teach a specific topic in a seminar. Today we get it done in two. The life span of

THE METHOD OF QUANTUM ENERGY

knowledge[6] is also shorter. With this new or increased energy, many things are no longer necessary. Today, much more is possible. The new methods are based on the statement that we are clearly able to do more than we dare. Albert Einstein said at the time that we use only 10 percent of our potential. He was just talking about our spiritual potential.

So, in the end, we might just use 4 to 5 percent of our full potential. When we finally realize that within us, we can do things that we have not even dared to dream, self-healing included.

The science, especially quantum physics, now demonstrates in experiments what many spiritual traditions have long been claiming—that everything is connected to everything.[7] So we are one, connected by an energetic field or energetic consciousness (more on this in the next subpart). For example, it explains the phenomenon when we are thinking of a person, and, the next moment or a short time after, the person is calling. So if everything is connected, then we can do things that others do too.

I even get a bit further with that. As the Bible states, God created us in His image. That means the Creator and creation is one. If this is indeed true, then we can create just as God created. Jesus healed people, and we, as human beings, can heal animals and plants too. You cannot believe it? Then you should quickly set the book aside. Otherwise, you may experience by doing many exercises that it proves the opposite. I have witnessed things and people in my seminars that even took my breath away. You may want to do a small exercise so you can see what you are capable of.

Maybe you are already familiar with it. Do you recognize the extraordinary in here? Or is it a given for you? This is the paradox that we have forgotten to recognize the extraordinary. If we were to bring a man from the eighteenth to our twenty-first century, he probably would not be able to close his mouth from amazement.

---

[6] The life span of knowledge is used to indicate how long knowledge is acquired in a formal or informal manner, in a timely manner (and therefore up-to-date), and the practice remains applicable. etc.

[7] See the principle of intertwinement (e.g., on YouTube, where many individuals upload and share their videos).

MAKE A "MIRACLE" EXPERIENCEABLE.

Stand up and stretch both arms straight forward so that the palms of your hands touch each other. The fingertips also point forward. Now turn both arms as far to the left around your body axis as you can. The feet remain where they were. Only the arms, the shoulder, back, and hip rotate. Note exactly your point of extension. Use the wall or whatever you can see as a reference point at the extension of your arms. Now put your arms back to your starting point, let them hang on the side of your body, or shake them a little. Repeat the exercise. Has anything changed? Probably not.

Now take a closer look at the path you have just travelled with your arms. The arms stay in the hanging position. Then close your eyes. Imagine now how to turn your arms to the left again. Envision them coming three inches further. Then go back with your arms to the starting position. Repeat the same exercise twice. Rotate your arms three inches further than before. Feel in your mind how your muscles stretch a little more, allowing you to move three inches further.

Here comes the test. Repeat the exercise. Not in your imagination but in reality. Could you turn your arms further than before? I assume you could. Congratulations, you are just witnessing your own little "miracle."

Rejoice at the miracles that can happen. However, these miracles do not happen by method. You yourself are the one who evoked the miracle; you are the creator of it. And if you can recognize this and accept it for yourself, the miracles will appear more and more frequently in your life and always will because you brought them into your life. Welcome to quantum consciousness!

Not long ago, I had learned that I should protect myself from the negative energies of my clients. I had to have specific movement sequences so that everything worked out, and it was important to remember spiritual helpers support. I had to pray specific prayers, but all this is not necessary anymore. Because when creators and creation are one, what do I have to protect myself from? For what do I need spiritual helpers when I am the greatest force myself?

I would like to mention an important aspect: I have bad news for your ego. It cannot praise itself for the great healing it was doing or pat itself on the back. We are the driving force of self-healing powers that are now set in motion in the other person. So the term healer, as generally understood, is not correct here. Nevertheless, you set a healing process in gear in a quite simple way.

This is what you will find again and again during the process. Today it happens much faster than we had learned it before.

A therapy takes so much longer because the process is simply another. Therapy is not bad—quite the contrary—but personally, the healing process takes too long in my opinion. Fears, phobias, or panic attacks can be healed within a few minutes, not a few years.[8]

Classic physicians ensure that symptoms are eliminated. Alternative healing methods, the old as well as the new ones, go much further. In symptom treatment, pain is temporarily eliminated with the use of a pill. The pain is only suppressed and will most likely return later. The new healing methods work on a different level. Due to the healing impulses, only light and information will travel to the body exactly in the quantity it needs to be self-sufficient to heal. More on this in the next subpart.

---

[8] In the book, you will find that fears do not disappear or dissolve. Only a change occurs.

WHAT EXACTLY IS "QUANTUM ENERGY"?

"Go a step further: Don't think. Know!"

The question can be answered in one sentence. "Quantum Energy" is an easy-to-learn and scientifically proven method to achieve healing and changes on all levels. It works fast, is highly effective, and sustainable. "Quantum energy" ensures order in your body's system—no more, no less.

Science journalist and bestselling author Lynne McTaggart describes in the movie *The Living Matrix*[9] as follows: The medicine of the future will be called an information medicine because it will ensure that the 'tangled' information in our body is restored to its natural order. Your body consists of Energy—sometimes dense, sometimes less dense. This energy is vibration and comparable with light and information. In the movie *The Matrix*[10] with Keanu Reeves, it's very well demonstrated. As Neo, at the end of the movie, recognizes that he is the chosen one, he sees his whole environment only as a field full of light and numbers. This is the information that scientists describe.

---

[9] *The Living Matrix*, Koha 2010
[10] *The Matrix*, Warner Bros., USA 1999

THE METHOD OF QUANTUM ENERGY

The world in Neo's view: only light and information

Diseases, psychological or physical pain, limited beliefs, or fears: all these are nothing more than "tangled" information. The original state has been changed through certain aspects. In many exercises, "quantum energy" ensures that this primal state—the primal matrix, as it is also called—is restored as it was before fear, disease, or pain.

Typically, you are born as a pure being.[11] As a baby or little child, you do not know anything about rules, ratings, fears, or guilt. Children conquer the world while playing. They just do what they want, assuming the adults let them. Then they start to learn quickly from Mom and Dad what makes them smile or gets them upset. The child learns what is good and what is bad. This "judgment" forms the first structure around their pure being. With every other experience they have, their structure is formed further. The original, pure information is beginning to get tangled up. The more structure they form, the more tangled the information will become. Imagine a soda can that would be used as a soccer ball. With each kick, the can deforms more and more. Some people are deliberately kicking their own can. We humans have a masochistic character and tend to

---

[11] In some cases, during the child's development process, in the mother's womb, some information has already been tangled up. More on page 47.

destroy ourselves. Pay attention how you talk, blame, or punish yourself. Maybe you are also a person who can accept and love yourself.

"Quantum energy" contributes to creating order from the disorder. It restores natural balance.

How and what does "quantum energy" work with? As described earlier, many of the new ways of healing is working with "new energy." Again, this energy is not really new, but, due to earth's higher and constant energy elevation or vibration during the last few years, you are able to achieve significantly more. In many cases, "quantum energy" works with an extremely high vibration. This energy is everywhere. When the vibration is extremely low, you recognize a firm substance like a chair, a car, or a human being. If the vibration is extremely high, then you cannot see it.

Many call this the energy of pure consciousness. I call it the "source consciousness" because it is the energy of the highest consciousness through which everything is connected with the source: God.

But what does that mean? I would like to take a short detour to quantum physics and then quickly go into practice. The scientists have been researching for a long time what "empty" is: the space in which there is nothing. Space, the air, up to the smallest detail, the atom. The atom has an atomic center. Many electrons orbit around this center. There is nothing in between either. Can it be that this great emptiness is really nothing? This "nothing," however, this "empty," serves as our cell phone radiation/satellite connection. So nothing is something? It is clearly a yes because "nothingness" is the greatest thing there is. This nothingness, or as it is often called, the equal field, the zero field (after Lynne McTaggart), the morphogenetic field (after Rupert Sheldrake) or the collective unconscious (according to Carl Gustav Jung), is the field that connects everything. Max Planck, the father of quantum physics, identified this field as early as 1944. He called it the matrix. This field is the greatest treasure and, at the same time, the greatest secret that exists. If, in this case, I speak of source consciousness, then I call it the same thing. Because this

THE METHOD OF QUANTUM ENERGY

energy or vibration is a form of consciousness, that carries everything and includes everything.

To get a sense of what I am talking about, please do the following exercise:[12]

---

[12] The symbol next to these and other exercises indicates that you will find the corresponding exercise on one of my CDs to the book. You can find out more about the CDs at the end of this book.

EXPERIENCING SOURCE CONSCIOUSNESS

Close your eyes and focus on your thoughts. Now, one of your daily 60,000 thoughts is going through your head. Observe this thought as it comes, stays for a short time, and then moves on to make room for another thought. Or does the thought just nest in your mind to cause you a headache? If it does, let it pass, and see how long it takes until the next thought appears. Stop, stop! Wasn't there just a short gap between the two thoughts? Yes, there was a short gap. Have you noticed it? Yes? And then immediately once again. A thought comes, stays for a moment, and then leaves. Now it is there, the gap, isn't it? Did you notice it?

This short moment, this gap, is the legendary "source consciousness."[13] Pretty unspectacular, isn't it? But it is just like that. Now increase the exercise. Imagine expanding the gap a little, as if you were pulling the two surrounding thoughts apart with your hands. Now take a closer look at the gap. How does this nothing feel? Pleasant? When I go into the source consciousness, I always have a feeling of happiness. That is when I realize that I am in the source consciousness.

Can you feel it? That is the energy that changes everything. "Quantum energy" works with it, not in every exercise, but in many. This information may be a little confusing, but soon you will learn

---

[13] Some of my readers wrote me that they were not able to stay long in the source consciousness. For many exercises, you do not have to stay long in the source consciousness. So, if you find it difficult, do not pressure yourself. Most exercises are easy to follow and to perform.

THE METHOD OF QUANTUM ENERGY

how easy it is to tap into this energy to evoke spontaneous changes and healing. When I first experienced it, I thought they were kidding me. Good that I did not leave the seminar at that time, otherwise you would not read my book today.

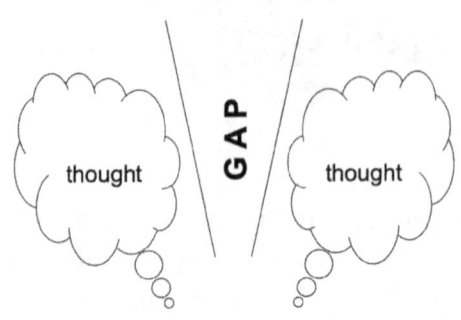

thought **GAP** *thought*

The source consciousness. The gap between thoughts.

I would like to share another exercise with you that may make it easier for you to feel the source consciousness:

FEELING SOURCE CONSCIOUSNESS

Rub the palms of your hands for a while until they get warm. Then hold your hands in front of you with your palms to each other and about twelve inches apart. Now press the hands together very slowly. Do you feel how a tension builds up the closer you bring your hands together? It is important that you do it very slowly, otherwise the hands are not sensitive enough. This energy is also the source consciousness. It is all the same.

Soon you will experience what is possible with this energy.

THE METHOD OF QUANTUM ENERGY

WHY IS "QUANTUM ENERGY" SO SPECIAL?

"If the mind understands, healing can happen."

Many people are enthusiastic about the new healing methods because they see it as a technique that changes their lives quickly and easily for the better. Often that is not the case. I quickly realized that there is more behind these healing methods than a mere technique. If you will recognize the full extent behind the supposed technique, a complete change of your lifestyle will take place. It will show you a whole new world. You will learn to be more conscious with yourself and the world around you. You will understand what health and healing really means. Your attitude toward life will change. With this book, you will not only learn techniques and exercises but you will also find out the reasons why your life has not worked out the way you wanted it to.

In addition to healing, "quantum energy" is also raising your awareness to consciousness. The more you know about the overall context of your life, the easier it will be for you to make the necessary changes. If you apply and use your consciousness of healing, you can quickly recognize the issues behind the problem. You will be able to get in touch with your soul to enter and dive into the depths and activate profound healing and change. Many people keep asking me how I manage so quickly to get to the core of the respective topic or problem. My experience plays a role, but, more importantly, I immerse myself in consciousness and let myself be guided by my inner voice. In these moments, I trust my intuition and just let it happen. You can do that too, with appropriate practice. In my other book *When Quantum Healing Doesn't Work—and Still Miracle Healings Happen*, I dedicate a large part of the topic to the consciousness awareness. Also, in my training to become a quantum energy coach, participants learn within the first two days how to deeply go into quantum consciousness. After that, they approach the topic healings and such.

Another crucial difference from other healing methods is that "quantum energy" integrates the mind into the work. I would like to tell you a short story. In 2004, Marcel[14] came to me with a blood phobia. When he heard the word "blood," he fainted. I specialize in the subject of fear and phobias and wanted to help him. After only ten minutes, his twenty-year phobia disappeared. After working with him, I tested whether the phobia had disappeared. I told him about a knee surgery with all its bloody details. Marcel listened. He was fine. But that was not enough for me. I needed to make sure for myself and poked a needle into my thumb in front of his eyes. Blood came out, and Marcel remained calm. *Great, the phobia is definitely gone*, I thought.

I talked to him about all sorts of things afterward. After approximately ten minutes, I watched the blood from his face disappear, and he became extremely pale—like in a movie. He had to sit down. When I asked him what was going on, he told me, "Siranus, I just couldn't believe that after twenty years, my phobia was so easily gone, so I just imagined how I could poke my finger." Isn't that unbelievable? After twenty years, Marcel had finally experienced healing, and, within a few minutes, he had gone back to his old state.

Our minds are extremely powerful. For this reason, I work with people not only on the healing level but also on the mind level. When we understand why we are in pain, have a disease, or a strange pattern of behavior that will prevent or hinder us, can acknowledgment and change at our mind level happen. I "make contact" with the tangled information. Every pain, every disease, every fear, every belief, and every blockage has a reason. I do not need to know the exact cause, but if I understand what all of this is for, I can actively make a differ-

---

[14] Name has been changed.

ence. You no longer need to fight it. Every fight is just intensifying it. More about that later. We want to achieve a change of consciousness so that healing can happen on a solid basis.

Earlier this year, a woman who experienced so much pain in her whole body since she was born that she was close to taking her own life several times came to me. Luckily, her fear of death was greater than the fear of pain. This woman in her midforties. Just by understanding what the pain she experienced was for and what it was trying to tell her, it was allowed to go. Without any other healing applications. Western cultures are very mind-driven. This is positive in many aspects. Without this expression, the Western world would not be where it is today. However, because of this strong aspect, minds have a great power over us. With Marcel, we have seen how powerful the mind can be. Quantum energy always works on the mind level.

At this point, I would like to introduce you to the exercise that "quantum energy" clearly distinguishes itself from other new healing methods. This is the "contact" exercise. In hundreds of my coaching sessions, this exercise has literally created true miracles. With its help, small and great sufferings, blockages, and fears were allowed to go, and much more happened. All this before any specific applications were used. I love this exercise.

This exercise makes it possible to integrate the mind into the work. But not only that. At the same time, it allows your manipulative ego to become a supporter. Isn't that wonderful? You can find out why your illness, your pain, anxiety, or your blockages are present—because everything in the universe has a reason. This is the natural law of causality. So your problems make sense. If you are sick or in pain, you are not just sick or have pain by chance. There is also a good reason to why you always encounter the "wrong" partner or have been repeatedly broke. Everything has its meaning. By "contacting" yourself, you will find out all about it. You will learn what the topic would like to point out to you. That is why its constantly showing up—to remind you that it is time to change your life. That is it? Yes, exactly. Or would you like to have it more complicated? Find the reason, change your life accordingly, and the problem will disappear. Why? Quite simply, when you change your life, the task of pain, blockage, fear, or what whatever it is can go.

In its simplicity, it is a miracle on its own. The next miracle will follow. Your ego, which annoys you so much, will change its focus from manipulator to supporter. Why that is, you will learn by reading the exercise below.

If you do not know it yet, your ego torpedoes your changes only because it loves habits, because they provide security. Your ego has only one mission in your life: to ensure your survival. It does a brilliant job. The only drawback is that your ego draws on your imprints and experiences from your childhood. He leaves the experiences out of your adulthood. All is exclusively based on your early childhood imprints (see page 108). Through the eyes of a young child, changes simply have a life-threatening effect. The mission of your ego is protection, nothing else. Even so, it may feel more manipulative and limiting in real life; to push the ego away or to overcome it is counterproductive.

From today on, use this exercise to deal with and get in touch with your problem.

MAKING CONTACT

Make yourself comfortable. Sit or lie down. Close your eyes and focus on your breath, as it comes and goes. With each breath, you will be calmer and can relax more and more. Feel how everyday life passes and you become calmer and quieter. Then focus on your problem (your illness, pain, fear, etc.). Can you feel the unpleasant perception that it generates? If not, remember a situation in your past where it hindered you. Can you feel the negative feeling it creates? Take a close look at it, and put your hand on the point where you feel it.

Even if it sounds strange to you now, talk to your negative feeling that represents your problem. Ask from within if it would like to get in contact with you now. There will be an answer for sure. The answer may not be verbally. It may be that you feel a change in the region of your feelings or see a picture. Whatever comes to you, allow it. If there is a negative answer or nothing happens, then ask yourself what you can do to make contact. Think about your problem. It never has been in contact with you before. Therefore, it must build a corresponding trust in you. If you are in contact, go one step further. Ask the feeling for its name. No matter what name comes to your mind, accept it, even if it is inappropriate for you or may sound incomprehensible.

Suppose the feeling is called Red,[15] then ask: "Dear Red, I would like to learn more about you. What is your purpose?" Or: "What do you want to point out to me?" Or: "What can I learn through you?"

---

[15] The name can be Dad, Steve, Fear, Lust, Pups, or a completely different one. It does not matter, because it is just a matter of addressing the feeling with a name.

Build a dialogue. Be curious about understanding it. The more curious you are, the more you will find out.

When you have found out what "Red" is for and what it would like to tell you, ask it, if you should follow its suggestion to make necessary changes in your life, if it would fulfill its purpose? If this is not the case, then ask "Red" what it still needs for the task to be fulfilled.

If it is fulfilled, ask if Red is ready to take on a new task. Mostly that is the case, but it is also possible that it just wanted to be free. That is fine. If Red is ready for a new task, ask it to support you. For example, if it originally wanted to point out that you should better take care of yourself, then ask Red if it would like to support you in this. If it is ready to do so, which is usually the case, make a "deal" with it. You take the lead; Red is just the supporter. Stay in contact with it until you feel "both" sides are satisfied. Then ask what it would do if you would not be able to keep your "deal." In most cases, it will allow you to keep the blockage, like in the past, because the original order has not been fulfilled yet. Something else may happen.

Finally, thank yourself and Red. After all, it has served you for so long. Then say goodbye.

Now focus on your breath again, and slowly come back to the surface of your consciousness. When you are back and present, open your eyes.

To ease the implementation of the exercise, here is the short form:

1. Go within yourself. Where in your body do you feel the problem limiting you?
2. Get in touch with it until you can feel it.
3. Ask: "Dear feeling, do you want to get in touch with me?" (If you have a no, ask yourself what you can do so your feeling is getting in touch with you.) It is important that the answers to your questions do not come from your head. Your head always has the correct answers—but you will get the real answers only from your feelings.

4. Ask: "What's your name?" (A term will appear. No matter what comes to mind, do not question it. Always talk with your feeling in the ongoing process with its name.)
5. Then ask: "Dear (name), why are you in my life?" Or: "What do you want to point out to me?" Or: "What is it I'm learning through you?"
6. "If I do what you point out to me, would I fulfill your task?" (If the answer is no, then ask your feeling what it is for.)
7. "When your task is fulfilled, are you ready to create a new task for me? Are you ready to take on to support me for the new task with all your strength?"
8. Enter a deal, an agreement, a contract with your feeling, under which everyone accepts his or her new task. (Shake hands, hug each other, sign a contract, or do something similar in your mind.)
9. Ask your problem: "How will you remind me, should I not keep my part of the deal?"
10. Thank it for serving you for so long.

That is it. Now it is up to you to implement your part of the deal even if you find it difficult. It is the action that will change your life.

The exercise "contacting" should always be done before a "quantum energy" session so that the subsequent transformation or healing, if it is still necessary, will be sustainable.

I would like to give you two examples of how effective the exercise is:

> *My high blood pressure problems are gone thanks to the 'contact.' It was a very impressive experience for me. For about eight years, I suffered from high blood pressure. I could only cure this with medications. Natural remedies and alternative healing methods did not work. After a few weeks or months*

of treatment with antihypertensive drugs, my blood pressure went back to normal, and I stopped taking medications for it. It did not take long, usually a few weeks, seldom two to three months, until my blood pressure was high again, mostly in stressful situations. I was severely restricted in everyday life. I grabbed reluctantly to the blood pressure drugs. In the fall, after a period without medication, high blood pressure was back again. I was desperate and really did not want to take medication anymore. I than 'contacted' my high blood pressure. It showed me situations where I allowed myself to be pressured, and it made me aware of my thoughts and words that I used. During this 'conversation,' I felt an enormous pressure leaving my body. It was an impressive feeling and hard to describe because it was unusual and so strong. I felt so good afterwards and finally had a great night's sleep. The next morning, I checked my blood pressure. It was normal! It has remained so ever since. This was months ago. In big 'stress situations,' I had high blood pressure again. Then I think about my 'deal' with my blood pressure, going back to the agreed conditions, and my blood pressure normalizes itself within a few days."

(Heidi Risi, Buochs, Switzerland)

The second example:

It shows very well what happens when you don't comply with your deal.

Since the birth of my daughter in 2002/2003, I have suffered from gum bleeding, which worsened significantly in 2011. I had a painful periodontitis treatment behind me, but this did not bring any improvement. The cause had not been addressed yet. One evening, I got in touch with my illness. It was little weird for me at first, but it worked, and it was amazing what I found out. (I must briefly mention that, at the time, I was still self-employed, which drained me emotionally and physically. My business was already set to close by November 2011.)

The disease told me and made me aware to become more reliable and to spend more time with my family. Aha. Me, more reliable? I'm the most reliable person I know, I thought. It turned out that I am reliable to everybody else, but not to me and my family. Oh my goodness! The closing of my business was scheduled anyways to have more time for myself and my family, which I wanted. Said, done. The disease and I made a deal, and we completed the contract. I followed the directions, and it would leave me alone. "And when I do not abide by our agreement?" I asked. The answer was: "Then I will annoy you further." Great, I was on the way to healing! I kept my agreement for half a day and fell back into my pattern. I thought, I will do it soon. When all is set and done by November, I'll have more time and do it then properly.

Ten days after the seminar with Siranus, I went to my gynecologist because I felt a lump in my right breast. After the examinations, it turned out that I had breast cancer. The diagnosis first came as a shock, but I knew immediately everything will be fine, and the seminar quickly came to my mind. I had broken my agreement, and I realized only I can change anything. With the help of God and my internal attitude, I can achieve an enormous amount of healing and change. Nevertheless, I have had some painful days, where the experience and the processing of it was a particularly important part. It took another six weeks before I decided which future path I would take. During this time, I had weeks of heavy gum bleeding, and my plan was to get my breast lump operated on. After that, I wanted to try alternative healing methods. At the hospital, I was told that my lump was bigger than expected, and it would require another surgery. Again, my plan did not work out, and my after-surgery care required radiation, which I really did not agree with. I did not want any of this.

I dealt with all kinds of emotions, anger, resentment, fear, sadness, anything you can imagine. It was also a time where people came up to me and told me exactly the right thing I needed to hear, to trust that it might be the right path to go.

After a night of very deep sleep, I woke up, felt free, because right then, I had decided that this would be the right kind of therapy and not what I wanted.

It's a nice feeling to trust, to let go and to continue to know, that everything will be good. That morning, as always, I went to the bathroom to brush my teeth, and the gum bleeding was gone! This has and still does move me. I believe and know that this was the beginning for my new life. Now I can say that I am doing very, very well after the diagnosis and even better than before. I have smaller breasts and currently must wear a wig since chemo, but I am feeling better than ever, despite all the circumstances. Most blockages are gone because I found myself. The time of processing my life, being with my family, conversations with awesome people, "quantum energy" exercises from a friend who was coached and trained with Siranus, this book, conversations with God, and a good supply of homeopathic remedies make me feel so good.

The path I am on right now is so completely different, and I am very grateful for my experience and to be able to share my story in seminars and lectures to encourage other people who are in a similar situation. It fills my heart so much when I reach other people and trigger in them a change and to give them an impulse.

(Bettina Greschner, Höperhofen-Germany)

With "quantum energy," you have a method at hand which works on the physical, intellectual, and mental level where healings and changes are possible holistically. You can achieve lasting, solid results. Another special feature of "quantum energy" is that it represents my essence of many successful methods. In all these years of my personality work, I have found that individuals react differently to exercises or methods. What works wonderful for one can be inconclusive for another. Therefore, it was important to me to use as many different methods as possible to tailor to everyone what works best for them. On the following pages, you will find specific exercises for your topics. I have a single goal: to evoke changes and healing quickly, easily, and effectively.

YOUR PREREQUISITES FOR SUCCESS

"Everything is easy if we only know how!"

After three years of coaching this subject, I know that there are aspects that support the success of "quantum energy"—for the user and the recipient. At this point, I would like to simplify it and call the positive changes "healing."[16] I would like to go so far to call the user that gives the impulse of the healing "healer," even though, scientifically, it is not a correct statement. Impulse-giver would be correct but sounds so mechanical to me.

So here are the prerequisites for the healer:

- Having loving devotion
- Having carefulness and respect
- Being able to be a driving force
- Being full of intent and free of expectations
- Always starting with yourself and protecting yourself in the beginning
- After completion of exercise, releasing the connection
- Constantly practicing to master your skills

"Quantum energy" can also be performed one time and be effective. It is a great method with a large-result spectrum. Depending on what is at stake, a lot can happen to you or your counterpart, if used on yourself or someone else. Depending if you use "quantum energy"

---

[16] I would like to point out that, in Germany, it is only legal for physicians and homeopathists to practice "healing."

on yourself or someone else, I recommend choosing an appropriate atmosphere in which you, as a healer, are in a positive mood, to focus entirely on your individual, work with loving dedication and mindfulness toward oneself and toward the other person. Be aware of what happens during this exercise. You are merely a catalyst for the self-healing powers you will release to your counterpart. I understand well that your ego would like to get credit for the outcome and success, because nothing would have happened without your help. But understand that your counterpart has healed himself. It is important to leave your own feelings out. This is not always easy, but it does not help the other if you are emotionally involved in the process. "Shared suffering is half suffering" does not apply here; it would be double suffering. Enjoy the miracles that can happen.

You have an intention: you want to heal. No matter what it is, the intention is important in this respect. You must be free of expectations. The healing process takes place in the way it should. What the exact result will be, you do not have the influence over. Explain that to your counterpart at the beginning of the exercise. That way, you cannot disappoint anyone. I have experienced a wide variety of things: from no result at all, over a creeping healing process, up to immediate massive effects. At this point, I would like to tell you two stories.

One happened during one of my seminars. I worked with a person on stage. I had fifty seminar participants in the audience. It was about balancing pain. Everything went well. During the healing process, I already had a strange feeling (but what happened needed to happen). No change in my individual. Can you imagine how I felt when having raved about this method and one hundred eyes were on me and saw that nothing happened? So I was breathing two deep breaths and started asking questions. After less than five minutes, it turned out that the cure could not take place at all! The person had a great benefit that the pain was present. To release her pain, she would have to do things she was not willing to do. So she used the phenomenon pain so she did not have to act.[17] All of this did not happen on the conscious but on the subconscious level. She did not realize that she used this manipulation strategy on herself. On the conscious level, she wanted the pain to go, but, unconsciously, she did not let this happen.

What a weird game we play with ourselves sometimes. It is the game of life, nothing else.

The second story took place during training as a "quantum energy coach." Two participants worked together. It was about the release of fears. The work process began, and suddenly one of the participants' bodies started to shake and did not stop. What had happened? Through the exercise, this individual's childhood memories came up that she had buried deeply in her subconscious mind. They were below her fear. During the whole process, her mind was totally clear. She was able to speak to us, but the emotions that came up made her whole body shake. The participant was guided through the process, and this childhood trauma could be released. Whatever you bring out with "quantum energy" always takes place at the right time.

Let me mention, what I mean by "always start with oneself" is aimed at the topic of "self-responsibility." Have you ever flown? When the stewardess explains the safety precautions, she explicitly states the following: "In the event of loss of cabin pressure, the automatic release of oxygen masks will take place. Please put on your own mask before you help others." How can you help others if you do not get air for yourself?

This also applies when healing. Always make sure that you are doing well. Only then practice healing.

The first time you work with "quantum energy" on another person, it may be useful in certain situations to protect yourself. If other person's energy feels strange, protect yourself. Imagine you are surrounded by a sphere of golden light that only allows good and positive energies to come through that are of light and love. This

---

[17] Elsewhere in this book, I explain how and why we have acquired such manipulation strategies and how we get rid of them.

energy will protect you throughout the process. Later, if you feel powerful enough and aware of your great creativeness, you will no longer need this protection.

It also makes sense to "disconnect" from the connection of the other person. Connections are constantly formed. To the cashier in the supermarket, for example. However, if you are working with others on their blockages, fears or such, a "residue" may remain. After these exercises, just "shake" your body, arms, etc. to let go of external energies. That is all you have to do. After a while, you will develop a sense of when it is necessary to do so or not.

The last prerequisite for a successful healer is practice. We know, in any sport, top athletes are successful because of their relentless training. It does not mean you have to repeat the healing process constantly. It is often sufficient to do a one-time healing session. I mean practice the healing itself. Unless you just want to use this book as a reference book for yourself or if you want to use *Quantum Energy* in "emergencies." However, if you want to change other people's lives, you need to continue to practice. You need a routine in the application of "quantum energy."

Prerequisites for the healer recipient:

- The greater your own confidence, the greater the success.
- Fear of failure affects the outcome.
- Be a doer and act.

If the healer acts attentively and respectfully, the individual that receives the healing can become more receptive.

My own recipe for success in seminars and coaching is that I can build trust very quickly. This trust allows people to open up, which is important for the healing process. This enables a much greater healing result. At the beginning of any exercise, ask if your client is familiar with the proceedings and if they trust you completely. If they do not, ask them what you can do to help them to find confidence. In many cases, people have been to many doctors, therapists, or neuropathologists without their situation ever improving. It is understandable that the trust or belief in healing is rather low. There are people who, mostly unconsciously, state that there is nobody that can help them—including me. My therapist, the only one which I would consult, quickly realized that I had an optimal prevention strategy for happiness and satisfaction. Unconsciously, everyone failed. Today I seriously wonder what I did at the time. But like everything in life, there must have been a good reason. Remember the story of Marcel's blood phobia? Our minds are immensely powerful. We are able, with the absence of confidence, to let the healing result be very minimal or none.

The same applies to fear of failure. We learn what happens in our cells when we are afraid and how this fear can prevent healing.

The last aspect is the actual action. This is where the difference is. At this point, you will find out if the participant really wants change and wants to be healed. For many clients, pain or dissatisfaction will be present again a short time after. In the beginning, I asked myself how this could be and if the method was not good enough. When I asked my previous participants if they performed their exercises regularly and complied with the "contract" deal, the answer was a shy NO. They had all kinds of reasons why they did not use the exercises or did not fulfill their deal. They did not take control of their lives after the exercises, and they continued just as they lived before. At this point, the cat bites its tail. If you want change or healing but do nothing about it, all effort is in vain. However, see these exercises as your chance and become active, take your life into your own hands as the creator you are, and your life will change—permanently. The process of "quantum energy" is like a triangle of understanding, changing, and acting! This guarantees lasting change and healing.

I understand why I am the way I am!
↓
I am restoring the original matrix!
↓
I am becoming active and recreating myself and my life!

THE METHOD OF QUANTUM ENERGY _____

THE KINESIOLOGICAL TEST

"A lie can escape your mouth—but your
body speaks nothing but the truth."

Take the kinesiological test (also called muscle test) before you perform any of the exercises. The test will tell you whether it is the right time, for example, to let go of a certain pattern, fear, or pain. Your body never lies, and we use this to bypass consciousness. Kinesiology says that things that are true and right give us great strength. Things that are not good or untrue weaken us. Keep your hands so that the index finger and thumb of your left hand form a *C*. Do the same with your right hand and fingers. Now place the fingers so you create a link. Press your left index finger and thumb and right index finger and thumb together. Pull on your link.

Now say "My name is (use your name)" and perform the exercise. You will feel that you have a certain strength doing so. Go back to the position and repeat the above statement, but now use a completely different name (so you are lying). Then try to pull your fingers apart again. Is it now (clearly) easier? You can also use other examples to find out if someone tells the truth or a lie. Truth gives you more strength than a lie.

That was the preliminary test. Now perform the exercise for the third time. Ask the following question: "Is it reasonable and appropriate now (use your problem) to let go/heal/or change?"

It is important that you are honest with yourself. If today is not the right time and you still do the exercise, you will be disappointed with the result. You need to understand first what this problem is good for and what it helps you to point out. It is important that you understand that this subject in the past was good for something. Recognize the positive within the problem, even if it does not have a purpose anymore and has hindered you more than served you.

THE FOUR AREAS OF LIFE

"Healing is always there, we just need to recognize it."

When I started to work on "quantum energy" and created the seminars, I did a day workshop. I called it "Pure Transformation." The participants were thrilled. It had so much concentrated knowledge that I soon realized it needed to be more than just a day workshop. Especially because I added more and more exercises. So I decided to create four, for all areas of life.

This was the birth of the following:

- "Quantum Energy Healing" for "Health"
- "Quantum Energy Relations" for "Relationships and Love"
- "Quantum Energy Success" for "Career, Calling, Success, and Wealth"
- "Quantum Energy Spirit" for "Spirituality and Your Life's Purpose"

This is exactly how this book is structured. Just look in the respective parts which topic is most important to you. You will always find something which brings you a step ahead in your own life.

Welcome to the world of quantum consciousness!

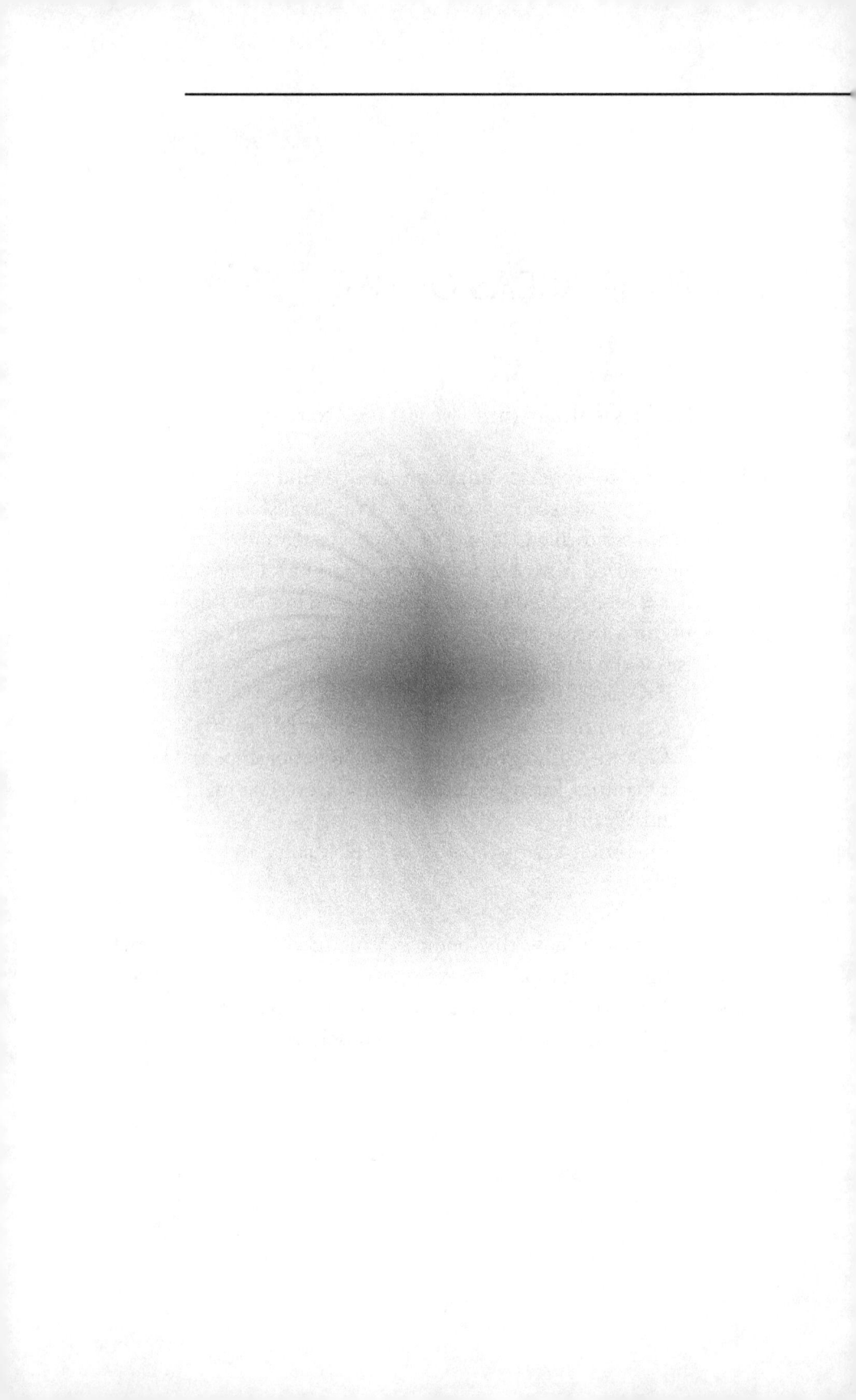

PART 2

Quantum Energy and Health

"Every disease has its purpose.
It wants to draw our attention to something.
Unfortunately, often we don't listen.
Let's start to listen to our body!"

QUANTUM ENERGY AND HEALTH

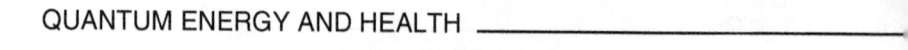

HEALTH AND HEALING

> "When we learn to direct our focus to what we want instead of what we don't want our life will change automatically. This is how illness becomes health."

Health is a natural state, every person's birthright. However, certain circumstances lead to the fact that you are everything other than healthy. In most cases, you create these circumstances yourself. Whether it is because you eat poorly, exercise not often enough, or are under excessive stress—you are 100 percent responsible for yourself. Only if you care for your health and feel responsible can you keep yourself healthy.

There is a law of nature that says that the energy follows the attention. You probably know it as the "law of attraction" or "law of resonance." At least since the book or movie *The Secret*,[18] this law is known around the world. It is a law like the law of gravity. It always applies. The quantum physics shows this very nicely in their double-slit experiment[19] in which an observer can determine the result of an experiment solely influenced through his own observation. It's hard to believe but true.

Therefore, you need to completely reorganize your attention. If you focused in the past on your illnesses, it's now the time to focus on your health. This alone creates healing. I realized a year ago that I was doing this automatically in certain situations. Always when I

---

[18] Rhonda Byrne, *The Secret* (Arkana, 2007).
[19] The double-slit experiment. More on this, for example, on YouTube or in the movie *What the Bleep!? Down the Rabbit Hole*, Horizon, 2007.

bump myself somewhere or experience physical pain, I quickly focus my attention to something completely different. What is the result? The swelling and pain disappears quickly.

Parents use this knowledge subconsciously after their child has fallen or hurt themselves, by drawing attention to something different. The child gets up and continues walking without crying or focusing on the pain. Most adults focus precisely on the point where it is hurts. The energy follows the attention, and the pain becomes stronger.[20] Try it out, and something will change, guaranteed.

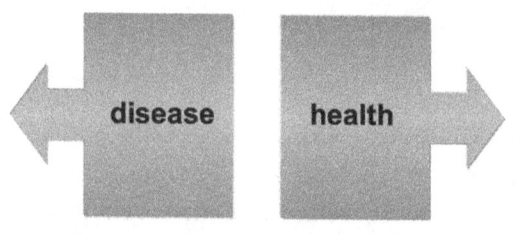

⬅ disease   health ➡

What do you focus your attention on?

"Quantum energy" always focuses on the desired result, which makes this work so successful. It's all about what you want and not what you don't want.

---

[20] Specialty clinics are now successfully using the knowledge to develop the so-called eliminate phantom pain in amputated limbs by using a mirror suggesting to the brain that there is no missing body part. The optical signal is sufficient "that the conditions in the cerebral cortex are back to the same condition before the amputation. (GEO, May 2010, 117–118. Page67)

HOW YOU CAN FEEL THE ENERGY THAT LEADS TO CHANGE AND HEALING

> "When in contact with the source consciousness,
> healing already begins."

I described the energy which "quantum energy" sets healing impulses with: "source consciousness." The contact with source consciousness makes it possible to bring the tangled information back to its original state, that of the original matrix. In the following, you will get acquainted and aware to this source. In this book, you will get in touch with the source consciousness in different ways. Therefore, I recommend doing the exercises a few times. Another exercise for the awareness of source consciousness is the following:

EXPERIENCE SOURCE CONSCIOUSNESS THROUGH BREATHING

Close your eyes. Just focus on your breath, how it comes and goes. Just recognize it without thinking about it. Just feel. What do you feel? Peace, quiet, security? Then open your eyes. Was it the same feeling as during the exercise you experienced with source consciousness? That is the energy of consciousness.

The more you encounter this source of consciousness and the longer you can stay in it, the more your life will change for the better. But more about this in the part "Quantum Energy and Spirituality."

YOUR BODY AS PERFECT SIGNAL GIVER

> "Your body should be sacred to you—
> without it you would be nothing."

Your body is absolutely perfect. It is made up of fifty trillion cells, assigned to different functions, all with the same code that include the DNA. Meaning, each cell possesses the complete information that your body needs to be fully functional. Every cell has a complete nervous system, digestive system, respiratory system, etc. Scientists have been working in Russia since the 1990s and have been very successful in regrowing organs based on this knowledge. One of these scientists, Grigory Petrovich Grabovoi, says: "There is a regeneration of lost organs possible because the information about the healthy organ is saved forever in an informative field." The physical human body is a manifested structure that results from the creation, using predetermined informational structure, a primordial matrix.[21] This is also how "quantum energy" works: the basic order—the original matrix—will be restored.

Every second, there are tens of billions of different processes happening in your body. These are necessary to ensure your life. At the same time, we only know a fraction of all these functions. A

---

[21] More about this subject in *Trilogy: Creation of the Universe* by Arcady Petrov, RARE WARE Medienverlag 2010. In these three volumes, Petrov describes in detail how the regeneration of organs and teeth is possible. Like my book, described in the first part, he writes about all the information the so-called quantum hologram or energy field that surrounds us. With the help of this information, the original state can be restored.

fabulously designed body to function optimally. For example, if you have a wound, everything will go immediately into action to heal it as quickly as possible.

Common colds generally take a week for your body to come back to health with or without the aid of medication. If something is wrong, your body will tell you about it. If you ask too much of it, it will make sure it gets some rest. This usually begins with barely recognizable signs, for example with feeling tired. If you do not recognize these signs or provide balance, over time the immune system will weaken, and the body will be more vulnerable. So it's not surprising if you catch a cold a short time after. This is another attempt of our body seeking rest. Because a cold is a little concern for us, and while there is enough medication to treat the symptoms, in many cases, we ignore these signals too. The immune system keeps shutting down, and you will get an illness that's worse than a common cold. Lots of people, especially managers, do not listen to these signals either and take stronger medications to not be absent from their job. At the end of these signals is burnout, stroke, or heart attack. All of these "illnesses" are the body's attempt to optimally care for itself. In this case, get some rest.

My father received, in 1992 at the age of fifty-four, for ignoring his body's signals, permanent rest. He died of complications from a heart attack. All because, because of stress, he ignored all the little signals at the beginning or perhaps wanted to ignore them. Which of these it was, I don't know. In any case, I have learned to listen to my body better.

Your body is the perfect signal generator. It is always focused on providing optimal care to itself. Learn to listen to it, and many illnesses and pain will not occur in the first place.

Now you might say that in today's economy it is hardly possible. I may agree with you. But let me remind you of your personal responsibility: you are 100 percent responsible for yourself, and you decide where you want to set your priorities. There are companies that send their employees home immediately when they have the flu. They do this because they know that they can only provide a fraction of their normal performance, and, in addition, the risk of infecting their colleagues is high.

FAITH AND HEALTH: A LIFE'S MODEL

"Pay attention to your thoughts because they become your words.
Pay attention to your words because they become your deeds.
Pay attention to your actions because they become your habits.
Watch your habits, for they become your character.
Watch your character, for it becomes your destiny."

—the Talmud

Pay special attention to this section. It's probably one of the most important of all because it shows you why you are the way you are. I will also explain the reasons in particular. This is what it is all about, "the life's model!"

As you have already noticed, your mind is very powerful. If the mind was programmed accordingly in your past, then you are usually in good health. If the programming was not so good, you suffer more often from pain, you are more susceptible to disease, fear, etc.

What does that mean? Quite simply, science is so advanced today that they can say our genes don't control our health, but our mind does. Cell biology, above all that epigenetics,[22] set new standards. As a result, you are not shaped or controlled through your genes but rather by your environment. Did you know that children up to the age of six are unable to make conscious decisions of their own? Their neural networks are not far enough developed for this. That means they unconsciously absorb everything that they experience through their senses. Their brain basically processes all unfiltered, so to speak. All they learn about health during this time, they

---

[22] Epigenetics deals with cell characteristics that are inherited by daughter cells but are not permanently in the DNA.

believe it's true. For children, their parents are like gods. All they say must, therefore, be true. What does that mean in detail? For example, the old biology perspective says if you live in a family where cancer was present in past generations, then the chance is very high that you will believe unconsciously that you will also develop cancer. Epigenetics says that this is not the case. If you keep hearing that cancer can occur in the family, then an unconscious belief develops in you that you too can get cancer. As we well know it, beliefs can move mountains. This deep-seated belief can lead you to believe you will get cancer. However, if you firmly believe that your cells are perfectly healthy, your cells will not change negatively. So your beliefs influence the cell information. I am not talking about conscious but unconscious beliefs. Positive thinking is here of little help in this situation. Why that is, I want to show you by using the so-called "life model."

Have you ever wondered why you are who you are and how it came about? How did your world develop in which you live in? I'm not talking about the whole world here but about your "little world" in which you move in every day. From birth and even in the mother's womb, you were shaped by stimuli that you perceived through your senses. You learned from your parents, your teachers, and the media about what the world is like (i.e., what you are allowed to do and what not, what is good and what is bad). You learn through experiences, develop beliefs, attitudes, and values. This is how you shape your world. Quantum physics speaks here from the "matrix." So your world is the matrix in which you are moving in every day.

my world

experiences, faith, limiting beliefs, values, culture, attitude, parents, teachers, friends, (Social) Media…

My world—My matrix.

With all your beliefs and experiences, you live every day in your matrix. So you're looking through your own imaginary glasses, one filter through which you view your world. Just imagine three people walk into a forest together: a botanist, a lumberjack, and a jogger. They all go through the same forest, but everyone perceives it very differently. Everyone sees the forest through their filters.

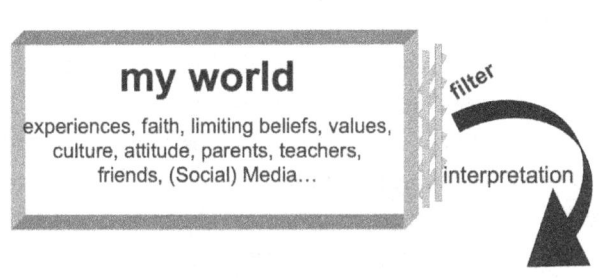

my world

experiences, faith, limiting beliefs, values, culture, attitude, parents, teachers, friends, (Social) Media…

filter

interpretation

""My World" filtered, interpreted through all my experiences and beliefs."

You look at all the situations that you experience through these glasses and interpret them accordingly. Suppose you lived as a small child in a family where the parents worked a lot and only had little time for you. So you don't get the attention, appreciation, and love you want. As usual in childhood, you play and get hurt. Once, you fall so hard that you get seriously injured. Miraculously, your parents are all of a sudden completely there for you, take care of you, because they are very concerned.

What do you think you will learn from this situation? Remember that in the first six years of a child's life, no conscious learning takes place. So you will get well, and your parents will go back to work. A few weeks later, something happens to you again, and you receive your parents' full attention again. So what do you experience in your childhood? Right, you always get the full attention and love when you are sick or injured. From this experience, an unconscious belief develops: "I get love and attention when I'm sick." This becomes an unconscious strategy and a behavioral pattern that will continue into old age.

Unfortunately, this becomes an independent behavioral pattern, and you will get sick frequently during your life, have an unstable immune system, etc.

But back to the life's model. This unconscious belief became your matrix, a habit. If you come across situations in your life where you don't get enough attention or receive the love you want, your unconscious mind looks through its filters, is interpreting the situation, and will probably do what? Get sick. Then look at your life, how it is shaped by your beliefs and behavioral patterns, and how it lets you run in your hamster wheel every day.

Another example: As a child, you experienced how much your mother suffered during her monthly cycle. Initially, you did not know anything about menstrual period but found out about it in school later. Years in, year out, you saw your mother suffering. What will your belief be about menstruation? Monthly cycle is normal and brutal.

Here too, your subconscious mind looks through the glasses and interprets the monthly situation. The body behaves accordingly because it had enough time to study it. This can be viewed as a "stamp imprint" in your cell information, a programming. The experiences shape your results every month. And so confirms your world, your matrix, your life: menstruation is something very painful. Subconsciously, of course, because we act unconsciously.

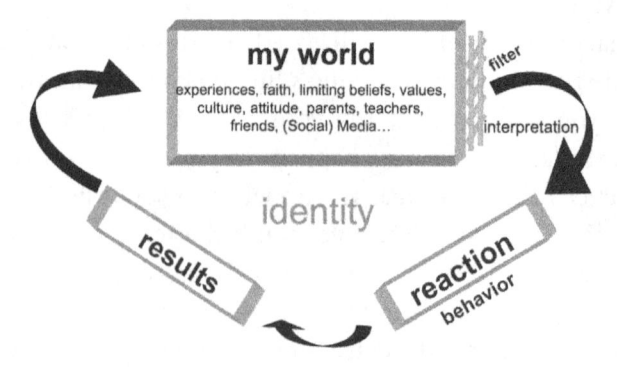

My world shapes my behavior and my results.

This is with all your beliefs. They are your habits. Look at brain research. It shows very nicely how a habit forms. There are billions of neurological networks in your brain. These nerve cords represent all our experiences, everything we have learned. In every second, there is an "infinite" amount of brain activity. Neurological networks arise when the end of a nerve cord, the synapse, is active and docks onto another nerve cord. That happens all the time. For example, it docks when we do something. Through the energy that it "fires off," it remains there for a certain period and will stick to this nerve cord. Then it looks for another nerve cord. However, when we do a certain task, repeat a thought, or perceive something again and again, then the synapse remains in the same place and is "glued" permanently. A new neurological network is created. We call this a habit. For example, you had to remember a lot during driving school to be able to drive a car: turn on the signal, switch gears, push the accelerator, operate the clutch and the brake, and, at the same time, watch the traffic. Today you do it automatically because you go through the multiple repetitions of neurological networks (i.e., the habit that formed). You now drive a car without thinking much about it, and you are even able to chat with your passenger.

What can you do to change your results so that you finally get or stay healthy? Most people do the following: they change their behavior. Look at the diagram of the life's model closely. What if you change your behavior? You react differently to certain situations because you changed your behavior and get new results. But what happens afterward? Your new results meet your previous world. So, for most people, the changed behavior works wonderful for the first time, maybe the second time, but the third time, the habit wins, and you end up in your old behavior again.

my (old) world
experiences, faith, limiting beliefs, values, culture, attitude, parents, teachers, friends, (Social) Media...

filter

interpretation

identity

different results

new reaction

changed behavior

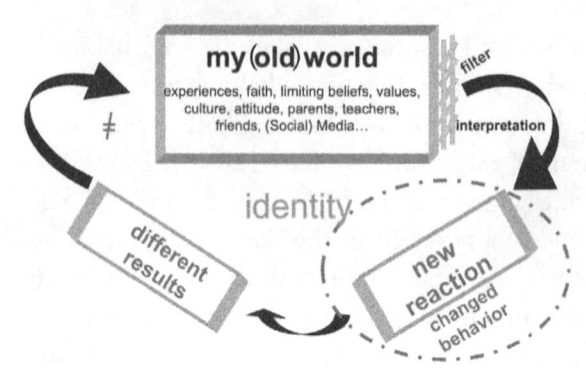

Changing my behavior alone does not lead to different results long term.

It may help for simple or light beliefs and emotional behavioral patterns to make this strategy work permanently, because the changed results will enable you to create new behavioral patterns. But generally—and you may know it well—you end up right back in your old patterns.

So if your beliefs shape your life, it will only make sense if you change your beliefs. That is the solution that is one of the secrets of life.

CHANGE YOUR BELIEFS AND YOU CHANGE YOUR LIFE: PERMANENTLY!

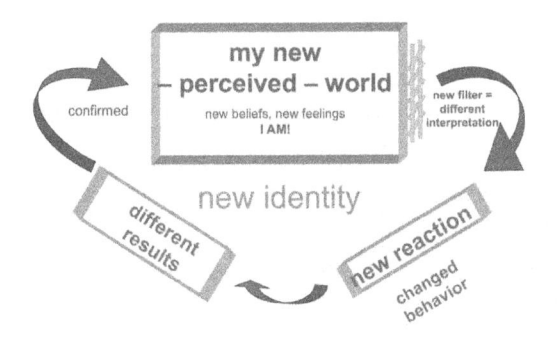

Changing beliefs changes my behavior. This leads to different results, and so does your outlook on the world you live in.

As in the double-slit experiment in quantum physics, a different outlook creates a different vibration and therefore creates different results. Or as shown in the life model, change your beliefs and you view the world through "new glasses," and you will reinterpret all situations accordingly. You will behave differently, you will react differently, and you will automatically receive different results. These other results, in return, will confirm your new belief. Ultimately, your world will change too.

Ask yourself this question: what are your negative mental beliefs or patterns that hinder your life?

HINDERING MENTAL BELIEFS/PATTERNS

Write down your beliefs.

Take a notepad. Write down all sentences, comments, or situations that limit or restrict you. There are hundreds of them. Many start with "I have to"(e.g., "I have to be careful not to get sick,") or with "I can't." (e.g., "I can't be healthy," "I cannot be free" (from respiratory diseases), "I can't go through a year without having hay fever," etc.) What are the statements you have learned—from your family, from doctors or through the media? Write down everything you can think of.[23]

My wife, Sonja, used to have almost every allergy that you can think of or imagine. Her allergy test had nothing that her skin wasn't responding to. You can imagine what her body looked like after all these tests.

The doctors made a fortune on her. There was not a week where she didn't see a doctor. This situation was extremely bad for her, as you can imagine. At some point she was tired of it. Without knowing it, she used the knowledge of quantum physics. She changed her beliefs and said to herself one day, "I can eat anything," which the doctors would probably have her advised against. She ate everything she wanted and had not eaten in ten or twenty years with pure joy and excitement. Something happened that nobody expected: she didn't react to anything. Since then, she got rid of most of her aller-

---

[23] In my book *Bring Light into the Darkness of Your Beliefs* (Schirner, 2012), I am exclusively working on unfolding and changing beliefs.

gies. In June 2010, she went back to the doctor and was tested again. Of all the allergies that she originally had, only three remained.

I don't want to recommend the same to you; but rather, ask the question of whether you are ready to let go of old beliefs and exchange them for new ones. My wife's example should show you only what is possible. A successful life in quantum consciousness means breaking free from old beliefs.

The next exercise will show you how you can gently change your beliefs.

CHANGING BELIEFS

Pick one belief from your list. Please sit or lay down. Close your eyes and make yourself comfortable. Imagine yourself acting with your new belief—not how you will act, but more so that you are already doing it. Picture this situation in all its details. Listen and, above all, "feel" how you act. The more intense you do this, the better.

It's best if you do this visualization every morning and evening—shortly after waking up and right before going to sleep—for seven minutes, thirty days without interruption. Should you skip a day, start over.

Pay attention to behaving in your everyday life according to your new belief. The more you integrate it, the easier it will be for you. It will become more and more familiar and will offer you the necessary security.

This so-called thirty-day exercise is based on the latest scientific knowledge of NASA. During experiments, NASA states that after twenty-five to thirty days of uninterrupted repetition in the brain, new and permanent neurological networks and new habits are created.

You will notice how your new belief becomes second nature. It may be that your old beliefs are coming back. That is normal. But you will recognize it and can decide accordingly to the new belief.

Why is it important to do the exercise after waking up or before going to sleep? At this point your brain is in the so-called alpha state. This state is like meditation—the mind and the body are calmer. So it is much easier to do the exercise then, and it will get into the subconscious mind faster.

An important aspect on the subject of "faith and healing" is the placebo effect. A placebo in the narrower sense is a dummy drug, one that does not contain any active ingredient and therefore doesn't have a pharmacological effect caused by such a substance.

In other interventions with placebo, for example, they do sham surgeries. The placebo effect is the successful healing without medicine or surgery. There are many examples in medicine. For example, in a group of knee patients, doctors opened knees during the surgery. Part of the group was operated on; the other group had the incision closed without having the surgery. These patients were not aware of it. All patients were able to walk pain-free afterward. The assumption is that more than 30 percent of all healings are due to the placebo effect.[24] This alone shows you how strong the effect of faith on healing is. What are you ready to believe in regarding your healing? The energy follows the attention!

---

[24] Gregg Braden, *The Divine Matrix* (Koha, 2007).

TRANSFORM PROFOUND MENTAL BELIEFS AND PATTERNS RELATING TO HEALING

"It is true: we are able to change our past!"

You have just learned an exercise that can help you to improve your beliefs long term. However, this presupposes that you know what belief is behind your emotional behavioral patterns. However, many people need professional support to find out what is going on behind all these patterns. There are also deep-rooted beliefs that cannot be removed from your world by the above mentioned exercise.

You seemed to completely be intertwined with that person. That is and based on our experience—again unaware we are convinced that this pattern is vital for our survival. Your body's system will do whatever it takes to keep the pattern active. You can visualize changes as much as you like with no results. Deep in your subconscious mind runs a sabotage program that ensures that no change will take place. Understandable, because your previous program believes you cannot survive without it. Remember: our bodies are designed to perfectly care for themselves. It will do anything to stay alive. As amazing our mind is, it has not learned to differentiate between different times.

Richard Bandler, cofounder of neuro-linguistic programming (NLP) once said in one of his workshops: "The great thing about the past is that it is in the past." He is right about that, but how often do we keep our thoughts in our past, although we cannot change it? This is a pure time and energy waster unless you indulge in beautiful memories that are good for you.

What can you do to change these old patterns within yourself? If you cannot change the past, are you powerless? Not quite if we use the knowledge of the new science. Why is it that our brain cannot distinguish between an idea and reality? That it can't see your patterns that were important in your childhood and now limiting you today? The answer is quite simple. Your brain doesn't need to distinguish because what we humans know as space and time; it is just an illusion. In my opinion, we created this construct to be able to understand day and night as well as the seasons and so on.

The scientists are very meticulous about proofing this in their research.

The principle of entanglement mentioned previously is a wonderful experiment that eliminates time and space.

But let's get back from theory to practice. You will notice that the exercises in this book partly take advantage of the opportunity to go back and forth between space and time. Not like a time machine, but very real. The next exercise is so powerful that it will enable you to change complete memories of your past.

If you can go through all your life's situations with a different belief, then all the associated subservient behavior patterns will change.

With this exercise, you will be able to change your past. Of course, you cannot undo the situations you experienced. But that's not important at all. What is hindering you is not the situation itself but the associated negative feeling with it! As with any insult or hurt, it's not the words that make your life difficult but the feelings that were created in you. For this exercise, you do not need to know what belief is associated with your behavioral pattern. It is exclusively about your feelings, not about any learned beliefs which, by the way, are called "negative beliefs" in psychology.

I call the exercise the "transformation of cell consciousness." This term describes exactly what will happen: the information in your cell consciousness will be overwritten.

The DNA is rewritten.[25] All your information is in every cell. We are transforming all your fifty billion cells. Before we start the exercise, I would like to describe to you exactly what you are going to do. At first it seems like a very laborious exercise. You will find, however, it will not take longer than ten minutes. Please don't do this exercise by studying or memorizing it. This is not going to work. Either read it out loud and record the exercise on your cell phone, or you can buy the CD "Transformation of the Cell Consciousness."[26]

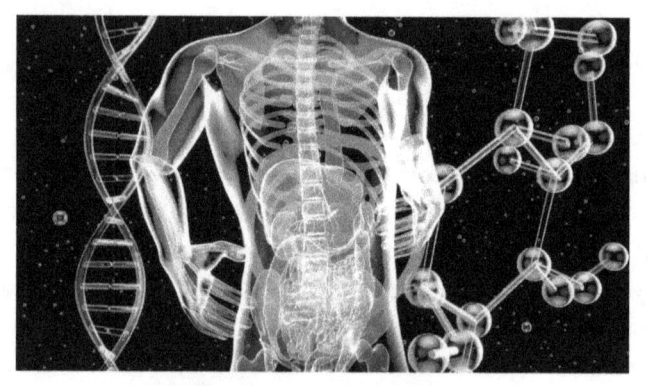

The DNA code is rewritten during the
"transformation of cell consciousness."

The Exercise steps:

- Have a notepad and pen ready. Write everything down.
- Look for the deep beliefs or the deep behavioral patterns that you want to change long term.
- Do the kinesiological test to see if it makes sense and if it is appropriate that this pattern can go.[27]
- Ask yourself the question "What do I want instead?"

---

[25] See also Bruce Lipton's "Intelligent Cells," Koha, 2006.
[26] "Transformation of Cell Consciousness" is available at www.quantumenergy coaching.com, and at Amazon.
[27] We brought these patterns into our lives to learn from them. If we have not yet achieved this learning, the time has not yet come for this pattern to go. That is why I place so much emphasis on understanding this concept in this book.

- Write down what you want instead.
- Do you remember a past situation where you already experienced this "instead" (even for a brief moment).
- Go back to this situation, relive it again, so that you are deeply into this feeling again.
- When the feeling is the strongest, clench a fist and anchor this feeling into your hand movement.[28]
- Take a journey back into the past through meditation.
- In this meditation, let your life go back from the present to the past.
- Whenever a situation arises in which the old belief/old pattern or behavior hinders you, place an anchor.
- Go through your whole life back to birth—in the speed that is right for you. (This usually goes faster than you think.)
- Relive your birth.
- Go further back in time when you still grew in your mother's womb.
- Experience the time of your conception. (Even if your head is now saying something else, it works!)
- Go back even further and experience yourself as a soul.
- Stay there for a moment.
- Remind yourself why you are doing this exercise, and get into the feeling of your "instead."
- Now make the decision to step into your life.
- Experience your birth vision.
- Relive your entire life from the time of conception to the present. On your journey, you will find all the anchors you have placed.

---

[28] The concept of anchoring comes from NLP. Many of you know the so-called Becker fist. Boris Becker (German tennis pro) made this move when he won Wimbledon, Grand Slam Tennis Tournament. With this "unconscious" hand movement, he programmed the feeling of victory into his fist and would later recall it again and again when he fell back during a match. With the exhilaration of victory that comes with clenching his fist, he immediately got his motivation back and caught up.

- Go through all the previously problematic situations with the feel of your "instead," and release your anchors if necessary.
- Experience the situations completely new.
- Feel as you relive the situation and how the cell information is rewritten.
- Go beyond the current present into the future just before the moment when you will die.
- Look back to the present. What have you experienced with the new feeling? What was your life like? What did you do?
- Then go back to the present.
- Come back to the here and now consciousness.
- Take notes from your experience during the exercise.

If you have not noticed many anchors during your journey through your life, that's perfectly fine. The unconscious mind takes and brings out what it needs. As with all exercises, the same applies here: there is nothing to be achieved. So rather be surprised with what will unfold, just like a little child experiencing the world.

Why am I going back with you before birth? Quite simple: often our imprints begin while we are still in the fetal phase. Even as a fetus, we notice what is happening outside (e.g., whether the mother is afraid, she is not well, the parents want or do not want the child). So there are already imprints in the child even before it has seen the light of the world. If the parents conceive the child during a phase of lack, disease, etc., this information remains in the cells during the first cell division. You can imagine what happens when these cells divide a million times. That's why we're starting before conception with the change. Also, for most people, it is a unique and beautiful feeling to experience yourself as a soul—a feeling that is not describable. Find out for yourself.

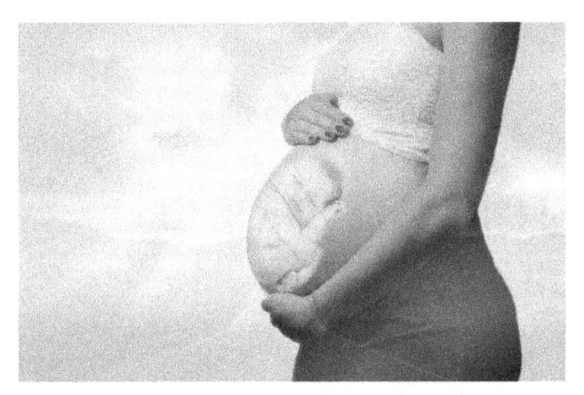

Even as a fetus, we are imprinted by our outside world.

The exercises "Transformation of Cell Consciousness" can be applied to all subjects that are limiting you in some shape or form from what you want to achieve.

Are you ready? Choose a quiet place where you can be undisturbed for the next twenty minutes. Have a notepad and pen ready.

TRANSFORMATION OF CELL CONSCIOUSNESS

Choose which deeply rooted behavioral patterns or beliefs you want to change permanently.
Take the kinesiological test to see whether it makes sense and if it is the appropriate time for this pattern to go.[29] Remember that it only makes sense to perform the exercise now if your body agrees to that. Otherwise you will be disappointed with the result. If your body doesn't agree, then ask the following question inverted: "What can I do to get you to agree?" Your inner voice will communicate an answer to you. It may come through a picture, a word, a sentence, or a feeling.

Once your body has agreed, continue. Ask yourself what you'd like *instead* of your pattern. If your pattern of behavior, for example, is that you are allergic to cats, the new behavior, your "instead," could be "I enjoy petting my cat, and I'm fine around her." Or: "Instead of being sick constantly, I enjoy living perfectly healthy all year round." What is your "instead"? Write it down on your notepad.

Do you now remember a situation in your life where you have already experienced this "instead" even if it was only for a moment? (You could never pet a cat without having a sneeze attack? Then use a different situation with a dog or any other animal.) Now close your eyes and go back in your memories. Experience the situation again so that you can feel it with all your senses. Meaning, don't see yourself like watching a movie. Be in the situation. Experience it

---

[29] You can find more information on the subject of kinesiology starting on page 36.

again—just like back then—and feel how beautiful it is. Get completely enthralled by it. When the feeling is the strongest, clench your left or right fist, and anchor the feeling into this movement. Relax your fist after a few seconds, and come back to the here and now consciousness. Open your eyes. How was it to experience this beautiful feeling again? I am always amazed what we humans are capable of.

Now get up, walk around the room, do something different for a moment, and sit or lay down again. Think about anything for a moment no matter what comes to mind. Now test your anchor; clench your fist. Do you feel that beautiful feeling appearing immediately? If that is not the case, then repeat the part with the anchor one more time until the anchor is placed. You should be able to achieve it on the next try.

Now off to the journey of your life: Close your eyes again, knowing that you have anchored your "instead" into your clenched fist. Your hands are laying next or against your body. Pay attention to your breath as it comes and goes. Feel how your body relaxes more with every breath.

Now let your entire life go backward in your mind. This usually happens very quickly, but take the time you need. You will encounter situations in which you fully surrender to your old behavioral patterns. Imagine how you place an anchor exactly at this point of your life, like you would place a needle on a map. Go through your adulthood, go back to your young adulthood, to your youth, to your childhood, to early childhood, back to birth. Notice your birth. Go backward to the period of growing up in your mother's womb, back to the time of your conception. Recognize your procreation and then go back even further. Now you are just a soul. This is where you stop. Enjoy the time as a soul in which you are completely free. Here is perfect, unconditional love. Here is all the knowledge of the universe, absolute peace and quiet, perfection in its purest form. You can feel all of this now. The connection to all souls in the universe—the oneness with everything and with God.

Even if you want to stay here forever, remember that you want to come back to earth to gather experiences. So prepare yourself for your life. Go to the room of visions. Here you will meet many souls. They will all accompany you on your upcoming life. They will be your friends, acquaintances, teachers, and more. Some souls are particularly brave because they pose themselves at your disposal by creating conflicts and arguments in you. These souls are so loving that they will offer themselves as mirrors to you and will bring out your deepest issues.

You may want to thank them now, because later, as an earth child, you will perceive this love as anything else than love.

Yes, exactly that is what they will be: the mirror of yourself.

Now focus on your birth vision, as you have imagined your life in all details, to get exactly the experiences you want to have. Realize that you first will experience exactly the opposite of it to understand later how important it was to experience everything else first. See your future parents and what you are going to learn from them. See your friends, your partners, and all the other important people in your life. See all their imprints that they will have on your life, all the good ones and the not-so-good experiences. They are all there to help you ultimately to make all the experiences that are so important to you. Every step is important. This is your ideal course of life. But be aware that you will often deviate from the ideal path. And that's a good thing too. Take a good look at everything—your potentials and talents, your preferences and passions, your gifts, and your destiny.

Now leave the room of visions and say goodbye to the souls. Now decide for your new life and see how that decision creates a vibration that goes to earth and is already taking care of your first imprint.

Recall the feeling of your "instead" by making a fist. Feel what you want and your instead, and get ready to immerse yourself into your new life. Are you ready to relive your life but now with a new behavior, a new belief, a new view? More free, more fulfilled, loved, healthier? Let's go!

See how your parents make love, merged with each other and just about to conceive a child: you! Feel the egg cell and sperm cell merge with each other. These cells already contain your "instead."

Notice how the first cell division begins, more and more cells are created, and the embryo develops. If your old pattern developed at this stage, replace it with your new feeling. If you need to use your anchor, do it. The cell information is changing. You are in the womb and feel how life force is getting bigger and bigger. You are looking forward to seeing the light of day soon. Then the time has come: the birth! Scream out loud and be excited for what is about to come. Now you experience your early childhood phase. Do you find any set anchors here to show you your old patterns? Then replace the new feeling with the old as well. If necessary, release your anchor. You will notice that you will experience all situations completely new. Your memories will change. Your cell consciousness is currently transforming, as if every cell is getting a new imprint.

You grow up from child to adolescent. All anchors will be replaced, all situations reexperienced, the cell information will change. Feel how your strength is getting stronger and stronger. You are grown up now, and you arrive in the present. Let life continue to flow into your future. Notice how you get older and experience a wonderful future. You enjoy your future to the fullest. Just before you arrive at the day where your soul would leave your body and your body would die, stop. Look at your last day, the day you will die. Realize that death is something completely natural. You were born to die one day. Dying is part of creation.

Death means shedding the shell of your body to enter as a soul a short time later into a new body. The soul never dies. Happy and fulfilled, you look toward the moment of death because you know you have achieved it all.

Now turn around and look back toward the present. What did you experience? What have you done with your new behavior? How did you live and who was with you? What special situations have you experienced that influenced your life? What have you actively done to achieve this? Take a close look at your timeline. See your new behavior pattern has completely renewed your cellular consciousness. Thank yourself for your life that you have created. Then travel back to the present. When you have arrived, feel your body. Feel where you are sitting or lying. Focus on your breath as it comes and goes. If you are fully back in your now consciousness, open your eyes when the time is right for you. Come back to the here and now. Take your notepad and write down what you have experienced. The more you write down, the better.

Welcome back to a new life. Life is wonderful, isn't it? I could always hug the entire world after doing this exercise with my clients or workshop participants. It's like a cell rejuvenation treatment that will change everything.

Enjoy the upcoming time. You may have already experienced and felt a lot during the exercise. Now wait and see what may happen. It can be a lot that shows up immediately, or it may be a little and it will take some time.

Your soul knows what is good for it. For it, there is no faster or better. Let go of all expectations, and enjoy what may happen.

GET RID OF FEARS, PHOBIAS, AND PANIC ATTACKS

> "It's not the fear itself that panics us. It's just the uncomfortable feeling. This is our redemption."

Many people come to me because they no longer know what to do. They are dealing with fear or have panic attacks for years that literally paralyzes them. Is that familiar to you? These people want me to erase or remove and "make these fears go away." But that's exactly what I'm not going to do. Fear always has something positive. It is pointing out something to people to protect them. Imagine I would take away a fear, and the next day you would go quite comfortably across the street without looking left or right. You can certainly imagine how this would turn out. That is why I will not take your fears away, because they ultimately ensure that you are careful.

Fears are archaic basic patterns that want to warn us about something. They give us important indications that something is wrong. There are only a few fears we are born with. Most of them we acquire during our life. There are different opinions what the basic fears of humans are. I want to mention three on which the others are building on:

- Fear of being alone/loneliness
- Fear of senselessness/absurdity
- Fear of finiteness/death

All other fears, we learn through different circumstances. For the most part, these are situations where we did, see, or heard something bad. Our brain links this "bad" with an uncomfortable feeling. So, in the end, it is not fear that paralyzes us, but the feeling that comes up when the fear arises. That is the same with panic attacks and phobias. Just imagine the fear comes up, but there is no longer a negative feeling. What do you think will happen? Nothing, absolutely nothing. You will recognize the fear, but you feel comfortable. Now you can decide what you want to do.

That's why I don't take the fear away from you but only assist by supporting you in dealing with the associated negative feeling and change it into a positive one. After the healing, it feels as if the fear is gone, but it is only a simulated situation, because you only stopped responding to it.

The quantum consciousness awareness means, in this case, to assign different feelings to the situations, as in the exercise "Transformation of Cell Consciousness" to change the vibration and energy. The feeling becomes normal, as it originally was before the fear existed. The original matrix will be restored.

Here again is a story from my wife, Sonja. (She has achieved and accomplished so many changes in her life that she is just a wonderful example).

Sonja grew up in a (public) swimming pool, literally, because that's where her mother worked at. Later the family spent vacations on the Dutch coast. She experienced a lot of time in this wonderful wet and really became a "water rat." That was, until the movie *Jaws* aired. She watched the movie, and, suddenly, with every minute, her fear about the ocean increased. (By the way, this movie had terrified a lot of people of sharks.) After the movie, she never went swimming in the ocean. Her fear of sharks had developed into a phobia. And because fear tends to be surreal (just think of jealousy), the fear was so intense that she would not even go into a local lake. Anxiety attacks are rarely comprehensive. So, for over twenty-five years, my wife stayed away from water.

Then I did an anxiety relief exercise with her. It generally takes ten minutes for my clients to get rid of the fear—permanently! Unless your name is Marcel, and you don't believe in healing.[30] So I worked

---

[30] See page 21.

with Sonja on her shark phobia in May of 2009. In retrospect, I couldn't really test whether the phobia was gone. She could watch shark movies after the exercise without any issues. Time passed. In June, we went on our honeymoon to Bali. We had a gorgeous beachfront and we both went into the water. That was unusual for me; for Sonja not so much because it was now okay for her to get into the water given she was accompanied. It was also helpful for her that she could see the bottom of the ocean. But what really amazed me later was when I saw from my lounge chair while reading my book that she was swimming alone back and forth between the buoys. But that wasn't all. When she got out of the water, I had a big grin on my face because she happily told me, "I swam out of the security area, and everything was fine." Shortly after, my mind remembered the phobia, but nothing happened. Although I immediately remembered the scenes and sounds from the movie, the images and sounds no longer caused a negative feeling. So I could peacefully swim my laps. After that, the images from the movie didn't show up anymore. That was three years ago. In 2010, we went to Bali again, and my wife was swimming as much and wherever she wanted—completely fearless.

Changing the Feeling of Fear

So that you can go through life without fear too, I want to share the exercise with you that I used on Sonja. Read well through the exercise before performing it.

GETTING RID OF FEARS

Which fear, phobia, or panic attack would you like to change? It's best to start with a smaller one. If it is a great or profound fear, I would like to advise you to work with an expert. Should it be treatable with the exercise I present here, it may be necessary to work on your fear prior to this exercise and to familiarize yourself to achieve change.

Sit in a chair or armchair, and make yourself comfortable. Close your eyes, and remember a situation in which you had your fear or phobia. Go all the way into the situation so that you can clearly feel the fear. Where in your body do you feel it? Locate it precisely. When the feeling is the strongest, imagine, like a camera, zooming the feeling out of your body, about an arm's length in front of you. Now the feeling is in front of you. If your mind cannot comprehend this, don't worry about it. Can you feel the feeling in front of your body, or is it still inside of your body? It is important that the feeling is in front of you because then you are disassociated from it. This means you are no longer *in* your feeling. This reduces the intensity of your feeling and lowers it and makes it more bearable. If you continuously feel the fear in your body, zoom it out again until you can clearly feel it at a distance.

Pay attention to your feeling for a moment. This is exactly what keeps inhibiting you. A feeling, nothing more. Which color has your fear?[31] Truly recognize the color of your fear. Now what is your favorite color? Imagine how you pour your favorite color over your feeling so that the feeling now appears entirely in your favorite color. How does it feel now, a little better?

---

[31] In most cases, people see fears as dark (e.g., black or gray).

Should the color shine even brighter, then change it in your imagination. What shape does the feeling have? Pay close attention to its shape. Now start changing the shape. Change its shape to the extent that the feeling feels even better. If you have found the optimal shape, keep it. Do you associate a sound with the feeling? If so, how does it sound? Change this in your imagination in such a way that it will be pleasant. What is your favorite music? Integrate it into your feeling. Is the feeling warm enough, or should it feel cooler? Change the temperature. Finally, the question of movement: Is your feeling moving? Feelings rarely stand still, but it is possible. Does it swing or vibrate? Does it expand? Reinforce or reduce this movement—always with the aim of improving the feeling. Then start very slowly to rotate the feeling, first in one direction, then in another. Which is more pleasant? Turn it further in the direction where it feels more pleasant. Then change the speed: turn it faster. What happens? Will it be more pleasant or more unpleasant? Control the speed until it feels perfect for you. You can extend or shrink the feeling or let it vibrate. Play with it. Try everything out until it feels pleasant or even good to you.

Do you want to get the feeling of your fear back now? Your mind probably says no because it is a fear. Please check your feeling again. Is there still the unpleasant feeling that restricted you a few minutes ago? Is it a neutral or even a pleasant feeling now? It is your feeling; it belongs to you. Now zoom it back into your body, back to its starting point. If your mind says "NO, stay away," there will be a hole left in your body that you would leave behind that needs to be filled with a new feeling. Most likely, it will fill itself up with a similar feeing, a new fear. Zoom your new beautiful feeling back into your body so that this does not happen. Feel again. How does this changed feeling feel in your body now? Take it all in.

Open your eyes, get up to drink something, or just walk around for a few minutes. Sit down again. Now here comes the test: close your eyes again, and go back to the fear in your memory. How does it feel now? Is it still heavy, stiff, or whatever it used to be? Most people do not even remember what their fear used to feel like. Should there still be an unpleasant feeling, repeat the exercise. Then take another test. Now imagine how you can relive the situation. How does it feel now? Does your feeling still inhibit you, or does it no longer resonate? Is there still anxiety or an unpleasant feeling left? If so, repeat the exercise.

Welcome to another miracle. Congratulations, the feeling of your fear or phobia is now a thing of the past! At this point, I would like to mention Sonja's shark phobia once again. It may be that your fear shows up again because your mind remembers it well, but you will notice that it no longer finds resonance but rather a new pleasant feeling.

> "My colleague at work was terrified of heights. Even a four-step ladder, she already had problems with. I did the exercise "making contact" with her, and, with my help, we changed the feeling of her fear, as we have learned it previously through you, Siranus. After the session, she drove home and could not resist to test right away her freedom to be fearless. She went to the Three-Country Garden, at Weil, Germany (Rhine River) and climbed a tower and was thinking constantly: *The feeling of fear doesn't come back at all.* She took a picture and sent it to me. I was so excited for her. It is getting even better. Yesterday came a text message from her stating, "I am on vacation in Ticino (Switzerland), and, without any problems, I crossed over three (!) suspension bridges!" She even sent me a picture so that I would believe it. This made me extremely happy." Judith Menacher, Efringen-Kirchen, Germany

ACTIVATE YOUR SELF-HEALING POWERS

"Good that everything is already within us. We don't need to learn it; we just need to remember it."

For some reason, we have forgotten to activate our self-healing powers. We do not need to analyze it at this point. However, we can reactivate them by using the following exercise:
Activation of self-healing powers:

- Think about the subject for which you want to activate your self-healing powers (e.g., "improvement of mobility," "healing of tissue," "healing a sick organ" or a specific body part).
- Close your eyes and focus on your breath as it comes and goes. Feel how you slowly relax.
- Imagine the desired health state with all your senses. It does not matter how far you are from this state at this moment. Say to yourself (for example):" Health is my natural state," "I am completely mobile," "My airways are free" (or whatever you desire).
- Dive deep into the source consciousness until you feel it is good.
- Immerse yourself in the feeling of being completely healthy. What happens when you are completely healthy? What are

you doing? How do you feel? How do others talk about you?[32]
- Feel the situation so much until imagination and reality blend together. Experience everything up close. Be the desired situation! When the feeling is the strongest, press a hand's index finger and thumb together for about five seconds, and anchor the feeling into your hand movement.[33]
- Give thanks to the already-fulfilled wish.
- Come back to the now consciousness.
- Write down in details what you have experienced. Test your anchor by repeating to press your index finger and thumb together. Is the feeling of being healthy reemerging?[34]
- Repeat the exercise at least twice a day for the next thirty days daily, but you do not have to reset the anchor.
- Let the situation flow more and more into your everyday life. Act as if your wish is already a reality.
- If doubts arise, activate your anchor.

The more frequently you use this exercise on different subjects, the better your body will remember its self-healing powers.

Activation of self-healing powers

---

[32] If you are already experienced, you can do so while you are in the source consciousness.
[33] On the subject of "anchoring," see page 36.
[34] If this is not the case, redo the exercise, and reanchor the feeling once more.

A reader used this exercise the following way:

> *For more than thirty years, I was unable to eat fresh fruit, nuts, or raw vegetables. I accepted my allergies. I am really a person who does not like to be restricted or limited. To be a good example for my children to eat fruits, I sometimes bit into a "green apple"—what irritated my mucous membranes in my mouth immediately. I never took a chance on nuts.*
>
> *Because I am a book freak and like to hang out in bookstores, I discovered the* **Quantum Energy** *book. Without reading much through the back cover, I bought it—and devoured it at home. It did not take me very long, and I ordered the CD as well. I started to imagine what it is like to bite into an apple. I smelled it, heard the crack while biting into it, and felt the juice running into my mouth. Whenever this thought came into my mind, I imagined this scenario. I thought about it constantly—before getting up, when walking my dog, or standing at the checkout line at the store. After a few weeks, I suddenly had a huge desire to eat an apple. I took one in my hand and could not resist biting into it with pure enjoyment. What happened next? Nothing, absolutely nothing! It was great. Since then, I can eat everything else again.*
>
> *(Andrea Glanzmann, Solothurn, Switzerland)*

STRESS AND BURNOUT

> "Empty your head from the junk of everyday
> life. Do feng shui for your brain."

Stress

The main function of the human cell is to grow and to divide. Another function is the protection mechanism: whenever something is wrong in the body, the cell protects itself. However, it cannot do both at the same time: grow and protect itself. In the growth process, the cell absorbs all nutrients such as vitamins via the so-called receptors. During stress, hormones are released that cause combat or flight behavior.

This is a relic from the time when we were still hunter-gatherers. Under stress, the cells are therefore in the protection mode. The growth is stopped, as well as all functions that are not used for combat and escape. At this moment, it is all about one thing: survival.

Important functions slow down such as the immune system and/or the mind. That is the reason we cannot think clearly when under stress. People who are permanently exposed to stress have a weak immune system and are therefore significantly more susceptible to disease. Anxiety also weakens the immune system.

If we want to ensure that our cells are permanently growing and dividing to generate and revitalize our bodies, then we do this the easiest way by eating a healthy diet, exercising to stay vital, and focusing our attention on the beautiful things in life. For example, several years ago, I stopped watching and listening to the news or reading newspapers. More than 90 percent of the news are associated with negative headlines. If I fill myself with these negative headlines every day, it will not provide enough nutrients to my body. It is that simple. So I take the consequences of not being up-to-date with what is going on in the world for the sake of my happiness and health. I can live with that.

Let us look deeper into the cell biology. For the cells to absorb information from the environment, they have receptors. These receptors are connected to proteins that connect the cell with nutrients. These proteins react to good and bad signals from the environment.

Good signals are, for example, joy, contentment, and love; bad signals are anxiety, stress, negative thoughts, etc. If too many proteins are imposed with negative signals, normal nutrients supply can no longer be guaranteed. Too many receptor locations are associated and occupied with negative signals. This makes it understandable why too much stress can lead to serious illness or burnout in the long run.

The first and easiest exercise for stress is, therefore, a positive balance, so that "positive" protein compounds are increased and can dock onto the receptor slots. You do not need a special exercise from "quantum energy" to do this. Make sure that you find short breaks serval times a day to recharge positively. In fact, a minute or two is enough. In the age of the new media, this is relatively easy. For example, go for five minutes on YouTube, and watch a cabaret or comedy video. Even if the comedy only turns your facial muscles into a slight grin, it is enough that the happiness hormone can dock onto the receptors. Or use the walk to the restroom to remember a nice situation from your life. This is also the advantage of the "silent place"—there you have your peace.

Here are two more exercises to help you get some rest quickly.

RELAXATION THROUGH BREATHING

Pause for a moment, no matter what you are doing. Breath three times deeply, right into your belly. Then breath normally for a short time, and again three times deeply. You can feel how you slowly become calmer.

DE-STRESSING/BATHING IN SOURCE CONSCIOUSNESS

Close your eyes, and pay attention to your thoughts. A thought comes and goes. Another thought comes. Notice the gap between the two thoughts? It is usually short. This "gap" is the source consciousness. Now image pulling the gap apart with your hands. Stay in this moment, and enjoy the source awareness. "Bathe" in this pure energy.

Another suggestion: Create time for yourself after work and take care of yourself. Let yourself be massaged, pampered by your partner, go out for a meal. Whatever is good for you, do it. One exercise that helps you deal with stress better is focusing.

FENG SHUI FOR THE BRAIN

Pay attention to your thoughts. Be mindful of what you are thinking-now! Are your thoughts positive or negative? Keep paying attention throughout the day. Once you realize that your focus is on the negative, change it! This will provide a breath of fresh air in your brain cells and will make you automatically more resistant to stress. Expand the exercise and include your feelings. Not only think positively but also bring your thoughts to the emotional level. This greatly strengthens your power.

Scientists have found that the electrical energy of the heart is fifty times, and it's magnetically even five thousand times stronger than the brain.

This is the reason why we are affected by negative stress. The so-called distress inhibits us, while positive stress, the eustress, inspires us. At distress we feel bad, and at eustress we feel good. So use quantum awareness to change your focus.

In the part 4 "Quantum Energy and Success/Wealth," you will get introduced to an exercise where you can positively influence your life within seven days.

Go back to the part "Faith and Health (page 47)." Of course, stress has also something to do with your beliefs. For example, if you have the belief in you that, to achieve success, you have to fight and make an effort, then you are significantly more likely to be exposed to stress than someone who's focus is less important to be successful or for someone that achieves success easily. In our performance society, success is often associated with effort. What are your beliefs about our work? Are there any that hinder you? Then do the exercise from the part "Faith and Health."

BURNOUT

The starting point for burnout is the production of the stress hormone in the brain. Stress is the base for burnout. If you look at the front pages of various magazines, then burnout seems to be in style. It almost seems uncool if you are not burned out as a manager. Where have we gotten to in our society? Where did our economy end up? Today more and more people in companies are doing more work. Their management is exposed to more and more pressure, must meet even greater goals. Working hours are getting longer.

Burnout comes creeping up. The first signs are poor or restless sleep, increasing dissatisfaction, irritability, lack of concentration, etc. Reoccurring headaches, including heart pain and feelings of distress in the chest (which can also be a clear signal of an impending heart attack), are among the characteristic symptoms, continuous muscle and limb pain, ear siren or beeping, permanent fatigue, and insomnia, even stomach ulcers. Pay attention to yourself, your partner, and in your environment for the above signals. Prevent burnout with the exercise and tips described above. If the signs of burnout are overlooked, the risk of a heart attack or heart failure is high.

There are still no clearly defined developing steps of the burnout. To me, the three following categorizations make sense.

Phase one

In this phase, activity and aggressiveness plays a major role. Those affected usually feel indispensable, perform excessively, and bring the willingness to do whatever it takes. Because there are no acute problems in this category, most people don't recognize this phase.

Phase two

Performance is diminishing, overworked and dissatisfaction are more frequent. Lack of concentration leads to increasing errors and, generally, to reduced quality of the work results. The result is withdrawal and distancing of those affected. After all, people lose interest in their work.[35]

Phase three

The pressure to perform seems almost unbearable, which often leads to addictive behavior of various kinds. Fear and panic attacks are the normality. The risk of suicide is increasing and enormously high. In most cases, the individual seeks only expert advice in this phase.

Be cautious, and do not wait until this phase. You do not read this book for no reason. Also, make people aware within your environment for these signs of impending burnout.

Burnout does not affect only adults.

According to a study by the World Health Organization (WHO), affected people are getting younger and younger. Media like the Süddeutsche Zeitung, the *Hamburger Abendblatt* (local magazines), or RTL (TV station) have already reported burnout in children and adolescents. The most common cause among the little ones is bullying in school. The symptoms are like those in adults but also lead to self-destructive measures like anorexia or self-mutilation.

Sit down with your child early on. Pay close attention, and be careful when your child is stressed and is mentioning having frequent

---

[35] Found at www.help-when-burned-out.de Here you will find helpful information on the subject.

arguments at school. The first and, in my opinion, the simplest help for healing is listening. Also, you can do relaxation exercises together. Meditation and imaginary trips are just a wonderful way to relieve stress for children.

RELIEF WITH THE HELP OF QUANTUM CONSCIOUSNESS

This exercise is simple and will help children and adults alike. Lie down and close your eyes. Place one hand on the center of your chest and the other hand on your forehead.

Now do you remember a situation in which you were totally relaxed and full of joy? Immerse yourself completely in this situation as if you were there live right now. Feel that nice feeling again. Just think "completely relaxed and free" and focus on your hands only. Anything else does not matter right now. Stay in this position until you feel it is good. Enjoy this nice feeling, and open your eyes.

To do the exercise with your child. Place your hands on your child's chest and forehead, and ask them to remember a relaxing and joyful situation. Let your child give you a sign when it is completely immersed in the memory. Think for a moment, *completely relaxed and free*, and concentrate only on both of your hands. Anything else does not matter right now. Remain in this position until you feel it is good.

Ask your child afterward what it has experienced. Promote communication.

This exercise has lasting effects, and you can perform it as much as you like. You will notice that something will change in your body. Let yourself be surprised.

For all the workaholics among us who think there is no time for relaxation, he comes the ultimate exercise.

THE RESTROOM MEDITATION

I assume that you will be using the restroom frequently during the day. Next time you go, use the time to bathe in source consciousness. No, not at the urinal, for the gentlemen among us.

Lock yourself into a stall for five minutes. If necessary, do your business, and perform the exercise "bathing in source consciousness." Then imagine how you will flush away all your tension as well. Take it seriously. It's the little things that can make a big difference.

You see, there is always a way out of stress and a possibility to escape burnout. Don't wait for your body to show you worse signs.

And most importantly, take steps to get out of the stressful situations.

GET RID OF ALLERGIES

"How comfortable do you feel in your own skin?"

Allergies are one of the most common diseases nowadays. Because allergies often arise very early in life, we need to do an exercise that completely changes the cell information. The most effective way of doing this, in my opinion, is "the transformation of the cell consciousness" because it contains all the information of the cells and DNA.

Do the exercise to help prevent your allergies and to allow them to go. Use in point 2 and 11, instead of your behavioral pattern, your allergy issue, and follow the exercise as described. You will notice that quite a bit will change. After the exercise, let your body rest and regenerate a while, and test in your own time how allergy-free you have become. After a month or so, you can do an allergy test at your doctor.

I would like to mention a special book. It's called *The Liver and Gallbladder Miracle Cleanse* (2011). The author is Andreas Moritz. Based on Moritz's statement, many diseases as well as headaches and body aches are caused because our liver and gallbladder are completely clogged. Of course, all has its psychological causes, but, according to Moritz, many of the symptoms can be eliminated by cleansing the liver and gallbladder.

From my own experience and that of my wife, I can confirm this. Even my wife's stubborn hay fever became significantly better due to the cleansing and the associated colon hydrotherapy.[36] For the first time in thirty years, my wife, Sonja, was able to breathe freely until August of this year.[37] That wasn't possible before. Now she does the cleansings regularly.

---

[36] Colon hydrotherapy is an advanced form of intestinal cleansing. However, the entire intestine is rinsed and emptied, which is not achievable with an enema.
[37] My wife had tried everything possible to get her allergies under control.

HEAL PHYSICAL PAIN

"Be grateful for the pain: It is an indication from
your body that you have to change something."

Pain is usually a sign that there is something wrong on the psychological level. Our society has come up with all kinds of phrases to describe pain.

If you are constantly thinking about something, the headache will sure follow. Or if you feel sick to your stomach, then this rarely has something to do with eating something wrong but rather that your emotional world has gotten into turmoil. Your body is once again the perfect signal giver. Try to understand what it wants to tell you.

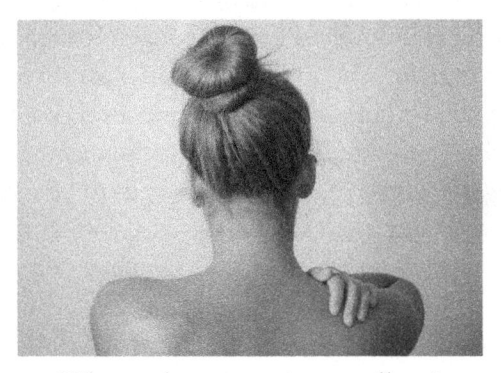

What is the pain trying to tell me?

You got to know an exercise which can free you from permanent pain by uncovering your self-healing powers. Again, your body is a great signal giver. Try to understand what it is telling you. A good exercise that can be used with all types of pain, especially in the case of new pain, is going in contact with the source consciousness. Here are some examples:

One woman reacted very strongly to mosquito bites. While most people get a small swelling after a bite, her entire body swelled up. After she learned the exercise, she immediately applied going into source consciousness, and, afterward, there was not even redness to detect after being stung.

A man complained of serve back pain. After the exercise, the pain disappeared completely. A woman had severe headaches. Her headaches went away after the exercise.

Healing does not always take effect immediately. Once, I invited a woman who complained of severe shoulder problems on stage during a seminar. I asked her, on a scale of one to ten, what her pain was like. She replied an eight. I worked with her. After the exercise, the pain was still a six. She sat back down in the audience. Ten minutes later, I asked her again about her pain level. It had been reduced to four, she replied. At the end of the seminar, the pain was completely gone. Jack Canfield, America's success coach number one, once said in a lecture: "Sometimes it takes longer." For example, a woman is pregnant with all the inconveniences that it brings with it. During the first six months, she had enough. No matter what, there is nothing she can do. The pregnancy will take three more months until her baby will be born. Sometimes it just takes a bit longer. This is how it is with the exercise of source consciousness. Sometimes it will take a day, weeks, or months for the pain to be completely gone.

Before we go into the exercise, I would like to point out something important: Do you know the feeling when you want to achieve something specific and you have an expectation, but it is not fulfilled? You probably know it well, right? Expectations are not always met. Therefore, it makes no sense to expect a specific result with quantum energy. My personal experiences range from great miracles to lack of any changes. It can range from a "damn, nothing has changed" to "wow, I did not expect that at all."

Everything is possible. After all, we enable only one's self-healing powers. Always remember, the body knows exactly what is important right now and what is not. Raising expectations puts pressure on you and the person who receives the healing. Should you leave everything now by chance? Of course not! At this point, we can rely on nature, in this case, the law of nature and resonance: what you focus your attention on is what you will create for yourself. Why should you not use the law of nature to give a certain direction to the path of healing? I am convinced that a firm intention will activate the energy that is needed for the self-healing. I experienced this a hundred, if not a thousand, times. For the following exercise, use a specific intention to increase the energy and give it direction. Where is now the difference between an intention and an expectation? This is quite simple: an intention gives a direction but not a fixed result. An expectation calls for a specific result.

Suppose you have severe back problems. Your intention could then be "healed." After the completed exercise, it may be that the pain has disappeared, became less, or that nothing has changed. Always remember: every pain has a reason, a meaning. Your expectation, however, would most likely be that you are completely pain free. If the exercise would act like a pain pill, the pain would have disappeared, and you would be happy to do your activities again. However, it may very well be that your body will bring back the pain because it wants to tell you that you should rest. So pain relief would be counterproductive. That is the difference. Be free from expectations, and formulate an intention.

When you describe your intention, pay attention to the following aspects:

1. Consider the law of resonance or the law of attraction. Is your intention "I don't want to have any more pain"? What do you focus your attention on? Right, the pain. So it most likely will become more than less. The statement "pain free" also focuses on pain. Formulate your intention in a positive way. Do not describe what you no longer want but

what you do want. The easiest way is to consider how the situation ultimately should be.
2. Always describe or name the desired state as if it was already fulfilled—not "I want a relaxed back" but "relaxed back." Otherwise, you will shift your intention into the uncertain future.
3. The simpler and, above all, the shorter your intention is, the easier the change is. The simplest formulation for all intentions is "transformed" or "healed," depending on what you intend to do.

Let us now heal the pain.

HEALING THROUGH SOURCE CONSCIOUSNESS

This exercise entails that you are already familiar with the source consciousness. Repeat beforehand the exercise "feeling source consciousness" or "bathing in source awareness." Recognize the gap between your thoughts now when the mind is calm. Now expand the gap to thirty seconds, to one minute, to five minutes. Were you able to keep within the source consciousness for so long? Wonderful. If not, you will notice that the exercise will become easier over time.

That was the pre-exercise. Now sit or lie down. Do not stand up, because it is possible that the exercise will literally make you fall over. We do not want to have any more pain than before, right? I will explain why you potentially will fall over.

Now place your hand on your painful spot. If this is not possible out of physiological reasons (e.g., because you cannot stretch your muscles sufficiently), find an alternative place, whatever works best. Then place your other hand on a healthy body part. Let your intuition guide you. It knows which point is the right one. Now go into the source consciousness and formulate your intention (e.g., "healed" or "arm is fully movable"). It is enough to speak out or think the intention. You do not need to make a mantra out of it or repeat the words. Then concentrate only on your hands. Everything else fades away. Hold the concentration until you feel a change. This change can be, for example, a tingling sensation in the hands, a change in temperature, a short tremor, or feeling deeply relaxed or similar. Or you just feel that it is "enough." The necessary time can be a few seconds but also up to twenty minutes. Experiences have shown that, in the event of severe pain, it makes sense to extend the time in the source consciousness. I also had situations where a few seconds were enough.

That is it. There is no need for more. Can you already feel how the pain became less? You do not need to repeat the exercise multiple times. Once is quite sufficient. You can also use the exercise with other people as well as animals.

The procedure is the same, except that in that case, you put your hand on the other person or animal. The beauty of it is that the moment you linger in the source consciousness, your own body is also healing. You will find that there is good in it when working with others and when setting healing impulses.

One of my "research groups" from quantum energy coaches has found that when working with source awareness, automatically the energy centers of the body, the so-called chakras, are charged. The group has been able to prove this with the help of biosensors.

Since the publication of this book, I have received a lot of emails from people who find it difficult to stay in the source consciousness for a long time or even finding the gap. If you are also part of this group, then simplify the exercise.

Do not try to find the gap; rather, concentrate the entire time exclusively on your two hands after you have expressed or thought of the intention. You will notice that you have no thoughts during this time. Should a thought appear, do not pay attention to it, and focus on your two hands only. This is how you can enter source consciousness.[38]

> *I was able to experience what "quantum energy" can do for a client with a severe facial second-to-third degree burn. The client has no longer any pain in his face. I have used quantum energy as immediate and continuous application and with the daily method and additional burn-injury oint-*

---

[38] In my book *Quantum Healing Can Be Done By Anyone—Including You!*, you will find some other options on how you can stay successfully in the source consciousness.

ment, which, in my opinion, seems to be even more effective through quantum energy.

(Vera Kissinger, Selzen, Germany.)

I could give you hundreds of examples of success, but I would rather mention a unique one to you.

My husband lives according to the motto: Do your miracle courses, but do not ask me to believe in it. So far, so good. Yesterday I got a back massage from him because everything was hurting, and I was very tense. I tried something with my husband. Since I cannot treat myself on my back, I asked him to hold a finger on the tense spot and another finger on a "good" place. In my mind, I connected myself with these fingers. No surprise on the outcome. He was extremely impressed that this tense thing (I do not know whether it was a muscle) was suddenly no longer there. He could press on it tightly without me being in pain. It was totally cool. What was most exciting for me was that I could experience it through and with him. So awesome!

(Nadia Ravljien, Mettmennstetten, Switzerland)

HOW TO HEAL INJURIES

"The most painful are the torments we create for ourselves."

With the help of pain, the body tries to get some rest. Healing through the source consciousness will enable you to significantly speed up the healing process. But do the kinesiological test first, if the time is right to do so.[39]

If the body still needs rest, an accelerated healing process may be counterproductive. Do not be surprised if you find out through the kinesiological test that the time is not right to accelerate the healing process.

The test was positive? Then, as in the previous part, perform the healing through source consciousness. Just extend the process. Stay in the source consciousness for at least eight minutes, or longer if you can. Wounds will heal faster. Even bones have healed faster after a simple fracture due to the use of the exercise to restore its original state-matrix.

If we allow miracles to be possible, they will happen. Think of the Russian scientists who are already able to regrow organs. Or Dr. Eric Pearl, whose clients have been cured from cancer or AIDS. One of my coaching trainees could heal one of his clients' cancer.

The time is right for us to heal ourselves—all diseases, pain, anxieties, limited beliefs, and behavioral patterns, etc. With this part, you have a lot of exercises at your fingertips which you can use to create perfect health. Again, I would like to mention, we all have these difficulties because our bodies are making us aware of something

---

[39] For the kinesiological test, see page 36.

(i.e., that we should better take care of ourselves or do something different). The healing alone is not enough.

If you do not make changes in your life after the healing, or pay attention to what your body is trying to tell you, the symptoms will come back. Maybe not in the same form but in another. Whatever the case may be, see your healing process as a first step toward a change in your lifestyle—and a more fulfilling, happier, and healthier life will be awaiting you.

Enjoying life.

ALZHEIMER'S AND DEMENTIA

"Our brain is like a muscle. If no longer trained, it will automatically decline."

Dementia and Alzheimer's disease have been on a strong rise in recent years. In Germany alone, more than 1.3 million people are currently suffering from it, with an increasing tendency.

What is the difference between the two diseases? Dementia is a generic term for the disease. It is the loss of mental functions such as thinking, memory, orientation, and connecting the thought content to the extent that those everyday activities cannot be carried out by themselves.

The most common form of dementia is Alzheimer's. Around 60 percent of all cases are caused by this. In this disease, certain areas of the brain cause disturbances of balance to the messenger, the substance L-glutamate, to the nerve cells, referred to as neurodegenerative dementia. L-glutamate controls about 70 percent of the nerve cells. In healthy people, the substance ensures that learning and memory processes can take place. In dementia patients, L-glutamate concentration between nerve cells is permanently accelerated so that the nerve cells are virtually permanently stimulated. As a result, (learning) signals can no longer be detected and forwarded correctly. The nerve cell cannot withstand constant overstimulation and loses its function and dies. The more nerve cells are affected, the more pronounced the perceptible mental deficits, the more they affect everyday life. In my opinion, it is only understandable that the more glutamate we use as a flavor enhancer in our diet, the more neurons are overstimulated and therefore may be, later, a possible consequence of dementia.

A medical reason for the atrophy of the brain region is increased concentration of L-glutamate. Another reason is that, when we outsource our brains work, memory also decreases. Nerve cells die, and regrowing cells do not survive because they are not used, says brain researcher Professor Dr. Manfred Spitzer.[40]

The computer, constant companion and helper of the people, is taking a lot of thinking away from us today. I still remember the time when I could do math tasks quickly in my head. When the calculator was introduced and, later, spreadsheets were added, I did not need it anymore. The PC took over for me. If I must redo it in my head today, I realized that it is no longer as easy for me. Spitzer calls this brain atrophy "digital dementia."

In children and adolescents, computers, Game Boys, etc. drastically reduce the ability to learn at an early age, Spitzer said. The consequences are reading and attention disorders, anxiety and bluntness, sleep disturbances and depression, obesity, violence, and social descent.

So much for the scientific side. What happens with these people on the unconscious, psychological level? The disease leads to that they can no longer actively participate in life. They withdraw unconsciously from the society and exclude themselves. What might be the reason for this? One possible reason could be that the family dynamic has changed a great deal in the last fifty years. In the past, it was a given that older generations lived among their children and grandchildren, and an appropriate intellectual exchange took place, and today the number of senior living facilities is rising. In direct terms, we are getting rid of the elderly. So it is no wonder that they withdraw and have no real interest in an active life anymore. In these senior living facilities, there is not much activity or exchange that stimulates their brain. Even caregiver personnel do not have enough time to interact with them.

The brain literally diminishes due to the lack of active exchange.

---

[40] http://www.br.de/fernsehen/geist-und-gehirn-digitale-demenz.de

An easy way to prevent or support treatment in the early stages of the disease is to actively train the "muscle" brain. Just as a muscle needs to be trained to maintain its muscle cross section to keep its strength, the brain also needs to be trained permanently. Make sure that your brain region is constantly encouraged to establish new neural networks. Communicate with others. Not just the small-talk style. Discuss, interact, challenge your brain. Solving crossword puzzles or watching quiz shows may be a first approach, but they are not really a solution. These activities are not sufficient in the long run. Take an active part in life. Get involved. Get your brain up and running. The longer and more active you are, the longer your thinking apparatus stays fit.

Even if the older generation is a greater task than the younger generation, do not leave your parents or grandparents in a retirement home on their own. If, for whatever reason, you are not able to keep them in your house, visit them regularly, and encourage them to exchange intellectual conversations on a regular basis.

If you are affected and have dementia or Alzheimer's disease in the family, I recommend that you proceed as follows: talk to the patient. Even if you feel that they do not listen to you, do not give up on them. Your words will reach them at some point. Be consistent. Always inspire them to discover a renewed interest in life. Show them how much you care, how worthy they are to you, how good the world is, and how much joy there is in life. Only when the sick regains courage and has the power to live does it make sense to take further action.

In one test, biophysicist Dieter Broers exposed several dementia patients to increased electromagnetic radiation. This so-called exposure of the brain region has enabled the patients to suddenly remember. The increase in electromagnetic vibration caused the brain to be stimulated again. This experience led me to develop an exercise to stimulate brain areas, to create new neural networks, and to regenerate neglected areas. Just over two years ago, I was working with a ten-year-old boy who was suffering from literacy due to a mental disorder. At first I did not know what to do. Then the idea came to me. I went into the source consciousness, connected with the boy, and mentally hooked on to his brain without leaving the source consciousness. I could clearly recognize that his neural connections were incorrectly linked. So I did what my intuition told me: I newly arranged the connections and left the rest to the universe. In a fraction of a second, I saw hundreds of nerve strands rewiring themselves within their order. After about a minute, all was good, and I finished the exercise. I gave the young boy a book to read, and he read like a young god: completely error-free and without hesitation.

We are now tweaking on these results, changing it up a little bit and projecting it onto dementia.

REACTIVATING NEURAL NETWORKS

Before you begin the exercise, ask your counterpart to sit in a chair or on the sofa and then connect with them. Get in real contact, and make the bond on the energetic level. Now put a hand on their heart, the other hand at the back of their head. Concentrate now only on your two hands, and you will automatically get into the source consciousness. Now build contact with the brain of the other. Imagine how you actively connect to the brain regions of the dementia patient. Take notice of all neural networks. Maybe you can feel the brain activity. For the exercise, however, it is not important. Focus your attention to the nerve endings, the so-called synapse. Think about the intention "activated." Stay in your intention for a moment. Then focus on the brain control center that controls the L-glutamate release. Do not search consciously; trust that it will find you. It will find you! Now enter the intention "regulate to the norm." Linger a moment until you feel that the synchronization has taken place. Then finish the exercise.

Depending on the condition of the dementia patient, you may have to perform the exercise a few times. Be surprised at the changes that will be taking place.

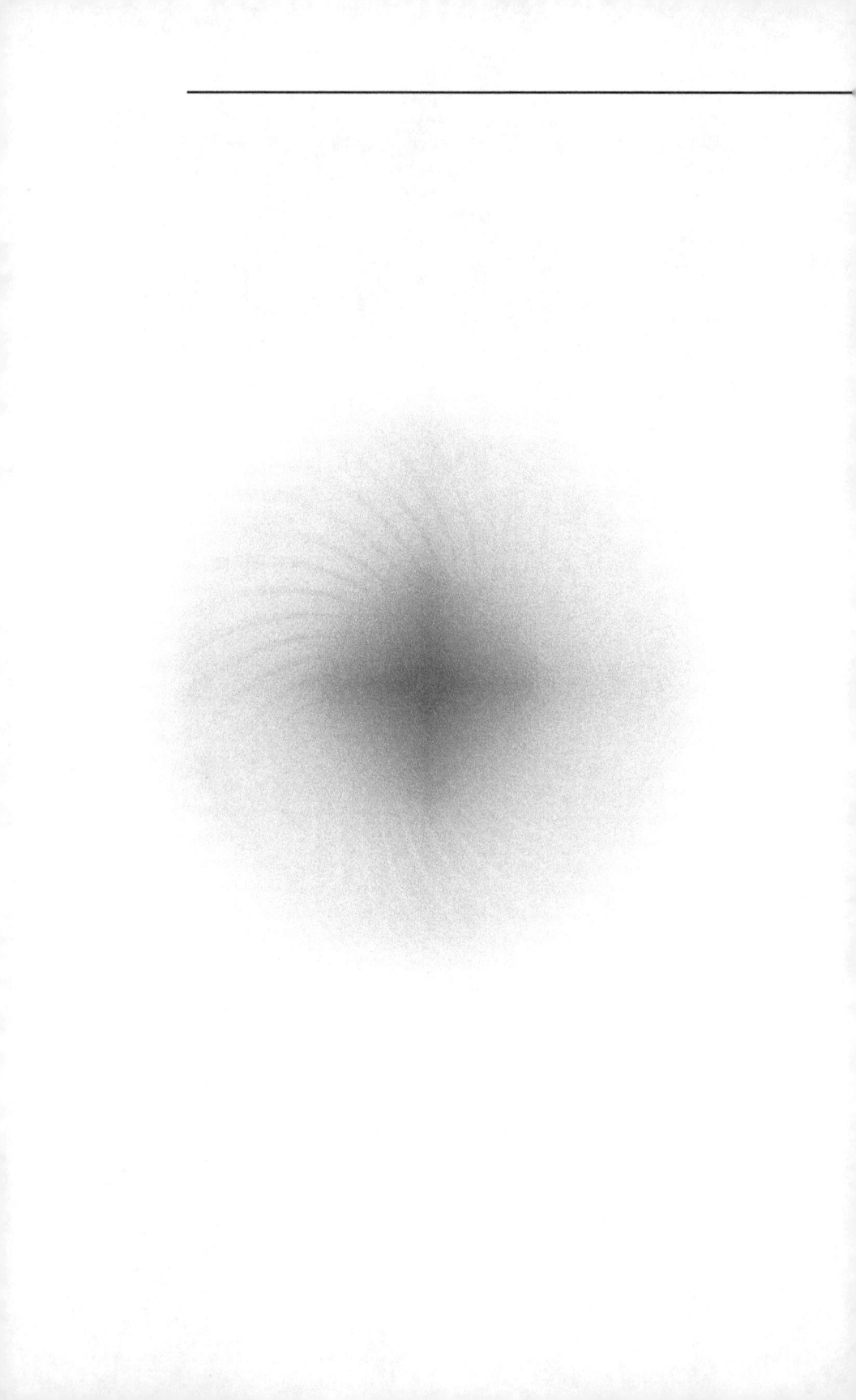

PART 3

Quantum Energy and Relationships

"Harmonious relations are a rarity in Germany."

I just completed a seminar with the subject "quantum energy relations." A whole weekend about the topic of relationships—the relationship with oneself, the partner, the parents, children, friends, colleagues, and your boss. As always, I am very touched because the participants left the seminar significantly changed. I realized how much the new knowledge will change their relationships and how much they have grown. These are the moments that confirm repeatedly that my work is correct and serves a purpose. Therefore, I would like to show you what you can do with the help of "quantum energy" to have fulfilled relationships.

Did you know that, in Germany alone, about one million couples separate per year, two hundred thousand couples divorce, and every seventh family is a patchwork family? Only 45 percent of Germans live in a solid relationship and a whole 2 percent in a harmonious one. A good seventeen million men and women are registered on dating sites. You are completely trendy if you have relationship problems.

RELATIONSHIPS AND HEALING

> "The moment we start to accept ourselves wholeheartedly, the gate of love will open. No matter where we will look, we will experience love."

I would like to point out one thing: first and foremost, relationship work means to work on yourself. Best described by Eva-Maria Zurhorst in her book *Love Yourself and It Doesn't Matter Who You Marry*: "If we can heal our own issues, then we are able to have wonderful relationships." In this part you will not learn how you can better deal with other people or what you need to do so that others can change. You will learn how to treat yourself better, take care of yourself, and learn to love and accept yourself. With the knowledge of quantum consciousness, this may be easier than you think.

Most behavioral and belief patterns, fears, and insecurities are the result of our early childhood experiences. If you want to have happy and fulfilled relationships, it is important to look back at what you have learned about love in the early years of your life. These early experiences—mostly unconscious—shape your relationships today.

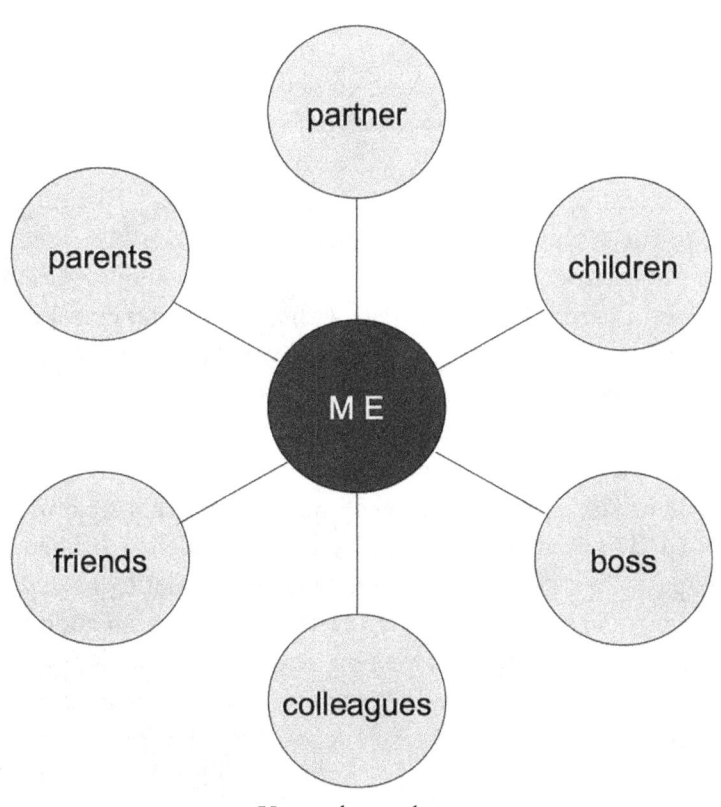

Your relationships.

YOUR RELATIONSHIP WITH YOURSELF

"When we do something good for our neighbor, we do far more for ourselves than for others."

In my coaching sessions, I often notice that a lot of issues clients come to me with are related in some way and can be traced back to the same cause: lack of self-love. Whether it is about relationship problems in partnerships, conflicts with a team member or boss, not advancing in your career, etc., as soon as we plunge into the depth of the psyche, we end up with the subject self-love.

Why is that? It's about our imprints from early childhood. A baby needs a lot of love and attention.

In our fast-paced environment, however, parents are often overwhelmed. The demand on parents today is completely different than in the past. Parents must be perfectly fit and athletic, make a good impression, and be able to manage everything. Through good friends of mine, I am currently experiencing this. Here comes a new family member, and it needs constant attention. The father goes to work, comes home in the evening, and the mother takes care of the child and the household. Both can hardly find time for themselves, which causes it to be dissatisfying at some point. On top of that, the child often cries, which leads to further tension. The baby is already aware of this complex, stressful situation and feels that something is not okay. It looks into the eyes or at the face of the parents and no longer finds the filled-with-love face, which it saw constantly in the first few days of its life. Many babies associate this with themselves, of course, unconsciously. They have learned that a radiant parent's face means "what I do is good." A face that is not glowing stands for the opposite. A human learns early on that he/she doesn't get the love he/she needs, and that who and how he/she is isn't good enough, even though the parents are doing their best.

Another reason why someone may be lacking self-love could be that the parents or grandparents came from a time when there wasn't much time for love. My parents, for example, came from the World War II generation. It was all about pure survival. They were not able to learn from their parents what love really meant. Therefore, they couldn't pass it on to me either.

If one believes the new science, it is already enough for the mother thinking once at the time of conception or during pregnancy that she does not want this child or cannot afford it or is considering an abortion to make the child feel unwanted. The mother can give the child all the love she has later, but this early imprint will still ensure that the child does not really feel loved or accepted. This imprint of not being wanted shapes the entire life of the child. Later, it will unconsciously choose partners who will confirm this pattern. The partnerships rarely last long, the person not feeling loved.

I had a coaching client who had exactly the partner on her side that she always wanted. Yet she was not happy with him. Her mind registered that all was well. On an unconscious level, her early childhood pattern does not allow that she can believe deep down that her partner is seriously loving her. This example shows how intense and gripping these patterns can be even when everything is there in the relationship. This again confirms that we act unconsciously 95 percent of the time and only 5 percent consciously.

Therefore, the first exercise on the subject of relationships is about becoming aware and answering the following question: "What have I learned about love?"

Take a notepad and pen and write down everything you can think of.

- What did I learn about love?
- How did I experience love?

QUANTUM ENERGY AND RELATIONSHIPS

- Could I "feed" on my parents' love?
- How did my parents live out their love in front of me?
- How do I love today?
- Do I have loving relationships?
- Do I feel loved within my relationships? If not, why?
- Do I recognize aspects of my childhood?

Get to know yourself in relation to love. Look at your notes. What did you learn about love? How were you imprinted?

Now let's go a little deeper. Put your notes down, and close your eyes. Feel inside yourself. How does love feel to you? How do you perceive love? Recognize your feelings. Are they more pleasant or unpleasant? Does love feel warm or cold to you? Write down all these feelings.

What have you found out about yourself and love? Is it a well-meaning partner to you or a stranger? The more you find out about yourself in relation to love, the higher your chance of healing through further exercises to improve your progress becomes.

"External relationships will heal automatically when the relationship to yourself heals." Those were Siranus's key words on the subject "quantum energy and relationships."

We as participants learned a lot and worked on improving and strengthening self-love and self-worth. These qualities were mostly a challenge for me. Life showed me this often and in a painful way. For example, it was never easy for me to talk to strangers. In groups, I often felt uncomfortable and not accepted. My fears often prevented me from entering new situations.

In the seminar, we were brought into close contact with our feelings, our deepest fears, and beliefs that prevented us from loving ourselves. We have transformed and healed a lot. All of this, including the good group energy, changed a lot for me and caused a great deal to open my heart. I suddenly felt how my outside world changed positively as well.

A few days later was a big festival in my town. I used to feel uncomfortable being there, but this time I could enjoy it, and I felt like I could be part of this community and celebrated.

I accept myself today as I am—so my community accepted me too. This is such a great gift for me.

A door has opened that allows me to be on every level, to walk on a completely new, easier, and promising path.

THANK YOU for that!

(Manuela Damman, Bad Bederkesa, Germany)

YOUR DEEPEST NEED

*"If we allow ourselves to be really honest
with ourselves, the heart is happy."*

What is your deepest need in terms of relationships? To be accepted, loved, to find security, to be understood, or to be able to lean on someone? What is it exactly? Look a little deeper: what is the fear behind it if you are not getting it?

Go inside yourself, and learn more about your feelings. Fear is a part of you. What would you like to do with it? Do you recognize that you don't want this anymore? "I don't want this fear anymore" is the statement that I hear often. Remember, the energy follows your attention! So what is happening if you no longer want the fear? Correct, it is increasing. So just do the exact opposite. Accept your fear as a part of you because it emerges in you. Imagine how your fear will be wrapped in a cocoon of love, and say thank you for being there. It wants to protect you from something, even if the protection is no longer necessary today. Fear has typically something positive about it. Right, I can hear you thinking out loud: "Should I welcome my fear for my entire life?" No, not for a lifetime, only until you find out what it is protecting you from. If you recognize and understand that, and if you have wrapped your fear with love, you will recognize changes within yourself over time. It loosens its strength.

I would like to mention one more thing about the subject of love. Take a closer look at how you lack love, and ask yourself the following question: "How do I lack the feeling of love?"

SELF-EXPLORATION: HOW DO I LACK THE FEELING OF LOVE?

Find a quiet place, make yourself comfortable, and ask yourself, "How do I lack the feeling of love?"

Your head is trying to find answers, but this exercise is not about an intellectual answer. It's about your feelings. Go inside yourself and feel.

How does it make itself noticeable to you? How do you feel it? Does it make you mad or sad? Where exactly do you feel it? Do images from the past come up easily? Just be aware and curious.

A lot has come to light these past three days of coaching that I've been searching for a long time. Tonight, I called in for a "men's night." I've invited my father to my house to thank him for everything he has ever done for me. I have always perceived his love differently and judged it because I felt I was missing something. This wonderful experience now allowed me to move on in my "own" direction. The conversation with my father was wonderful—and not like usual. No, this time was completely different—loving, calm, and understanding. For two hours, I sat at a table with my father and talked about many things—feelings, thoughts, and memories of the past. It was an incredibly liberating conversation. My father, while usually holding back his feelings and thoughts, was open and told me about

> *his feelings and worries. I felt my inner strength and love for him, which I typically express to him in anger and hatred. A deep wound was allowed to heal.*
>
> (Patrick Marquardt, Mülheim, Germany)

Would you like to find out more about yourself and the subject of love? Then I invite you to dive even deeper into your inner mystery and get in touch with your inner child. The inner child is the little boy or girl in you that never grew up. Everyone has this inner child. That inner child is that which behaves from early childhood. It acts according to the early childhood patterns because it has stayed young and will forever stay young. It retains the emotions that were dominant when you were a toddler.

If you were often sad or angry, reacted reluctantly, this can be a feeling that resulted from your childhood. The inner child holds on to these feelings until they are changed.

> The child portion of your personality categorizes all life situations and focuses on those parts that responded to that particular emotion. It forces you to generate thought patterns that create that emotion. On an emotional level, this part never left home. It's still there, waiting for loving acceptance and the unconditional love that was never received.[41]

---

[41] A. Samuels and E. Lukan, *In Harmony with the Inner Child* (Herder, 2007).

The inner child in us acts according to early childhood patterns.

When you go into contact with your inner child, it will feel seen and recognized for the first time. This is exactly what it desires so badly. By accepting and loving these feelings in you, the healing process begins. The following exercise will support you.

HEAL YOUR INNER CHILD

Again, find a cozy place where you can be undisturbed. Make yourself comfortable, and close your eyes. Take a few deep breaths, and feel how you relax more and more with each breath. If thoughts come up that might prevent you from doing this exercise, imagine these thoughts are like clouds in the sky. They come, pass by, and go. A thought comes, passes by, and goes—like the "gap," the source of consciousness. Now imagine yourself being that little kid again that you once were. Do you remember the time when you were younger than six years old—not a certain situation, only the time? Immerse yourself in this feeling. How are you doing at that time? Are you sad, shy, or angry? No matter what emotion is present, let it come up. You don't need to have a dialog with your inner child now either. Just recognize the emotion.

Now imagine how you, as an adult, place your inner child on your lap, giving him/her all your attention and wrapping your arms around him/her. Give him/her all your love that you carry within you. Can't find love? Then remember a situation in your life where you felt love. Now pass this love onto your inner child. That's what he/she never got back then.

What is happening to your inner child now? Is he/she smiling, or is he/she still angry or sad? Give him/her all your love, if you can; the longer the better. He/she is completely starved of love. Can you feel how the tension in the child is lessening?

Ask what he/she needs right now, and give him/her that as much and as intensely as you can. If you cannot do it at this moment, explain why.

When you feel it's "enough" for now, say goodbye to your inner child, and let him/her know what a great being he/she is. Tell him/her that you will be back in contact soon. Breathe deeply in and out, and come back to your "now" consciousness.

Don't expect an immediate change. Repeat this exercise often. You will find that the more you get in contact with your inner child, the healing will increase, and your inner child will be open to receive love.

HEALING LOVE WITH THE SUPPORT OF SOURCE CONSCIOUSNESS

You can expand the exercise when working with your inner child with the following exercise, and it can be used independently of the inner child exercise.

Incorporate this exercise when in contact with the inner child. The moment you give your inner child all the love, go with your attention into source consciousness, and let the love flow into the source consciousness. Hold the vibration of love and consciousness if you can. When you feel that everything is good, see what happens to your inner child. Say goodbye now. Take a few deep breaths, and come back to the now awareness.

If you do the exercise without the inner child, proceed as follows: Let the thought *love flows and multiplies* come to your mind. Go with all your attention into the source consciousness. Feel how you immerse yourself in it. As you hold the vibration of awareness, and the energy of love flows from your heart, image how a green or pink light rises from your heart and merges with source consciousness. Hold this energy upright for two to seven minutes and then come back into your now consciousness.

Be surprised by the changes that will occur immediately or soon.

However, don't have any expectations, as they can easily disappoint.

PAIN OR JOY?

Look in the mirror: What do you see?

As in the part "Quantum Energy and Health," I would like to ask you the following question: "Where is your focus and attention within your relationships?"

- Do you see the aspects that bring joy or those that do not work?
- What do you see when you look in the mirror? The beautiful things about yourself or the flaws?
- When you think about your partner, your parents, children, colleagues, friends, etc., what's the first thing that comes to mind?
- In your partner relationship, do you focus on suffering or joy?

QUANTUM ENERGY AND RELATIONSHIPS

For many, the big challenge is to love the reflection in the mirror.

Add to your list of subjects. What do you focus on? The energy follows the attention. What you focus on is what you create—that is an irrevocable law of attraction. So ask yourself what you are doing in your relationships and what you want to create. Use your quantum consciousness, and direct your new focus to it.

THE LOVE DIARY

Do you already keep a diary? No matter if you answer with a yes or no, get one or another one! Take notes of the following every night before you go to bed:

1. What did I do for myself today to make me feel good? How and with what did I take care of myself?
2. How did I "fill up myself" today in my partnership?[42]
3. What have I done today for my partnership so that love can grow and flourish?
4. How do I feel about myself and my partnership?
5. What have I done today for other people around me (parents, children, friends, colleagues, cashiers, bosses, etc.) to put a smile on their faces?

The more you focus your attention, thoughts, feelings, on positive things in your relationships, the more will change.

---

[42] Have you made sure that you are getting what you wish and been looking for in your relationship? "Filling yourself up" means asking the other person what love and attention you need, actively taking care of what you need. Most people starve in their relationship for love, physical contact, security, etc. because they don't demand it. Let the other person know, and find solutions together how you can both "fill yourself up." But it's not about taking advantage of the other; it's about telling them what is important to you in the relationship and what you need without applying pressure.

YOUR WORST TRAUMAS

"If we can change our past, even the worst traumas are allowed to go."

At this point, I would like to address a topic that is a taboo subject for many people: abuse. Since I have been a personal coach, I have met an infinite number of people, men and women, who were abused in their childhood. Not always sexual abuse. Constant physical or emotional abuse creates trauma in a young child. Since most abuse is kept a secret, many victims don't address the issue because they are scared or ashamed. The number of unreported cases in households are much higher than the statistics show.

"We are terrified that the past would repeat itself, especially if we experienced real trauma as children." Physical, sexual, and emotional abuse are one of the toughest problems an adult must deal with. Such experiences make us face the most discouraging, devastating, painful, and heartbreaking challenges. They rob us of our self-esteem, and life without self-esteem is an endless struggle. Such events are deeply rooted in our memories and prevent us from progressing.[43]

In my seminar "Quantum Energy Relations—Living Fulfilling Relationships," typically 60 percent of my participants suffer in their relationships and 80 percent have decreased self-esteem. In many cases, abuse is the cause. These beliefs about life emerged from it and could be as follows:

- "I'm not worth loving."
- "I am of no use."
- "I can't do that anyway."

---

[43] S. Simon, *The Power Is within You* (Amra, 2008).

- "I have to do something to be loved and/or recognized."
- "I am only a good person when I am nice and well-behaved."
- "I have to be perfect."
- "I have to submit to the masculine."

Do you recognize yourself? I could list over a hundred other beliefs or scenarios that arise from such abuse. All these beliefs shape your life and make it what you experience today.

How can these traumas be healed? One possibility would be to change the resulting beliefs. As you may have noticed, this subject goes much deeper. The so-called Sisyphean work would only scratch the surface. Even the exercise "freeing yourself from fears," which you may have already experienced, is enormously powerful but rarely enough for abuse trauma. You need to start on a deeper level to emotionally transform childhood experiences. You know the exercise already. More on that in the next section.

TRANSFORM YOUR BEHAVIORAL PATTERNS IN RELATION TO LOVE

"Be in love with yourself so that others can love you too."

After you have studied this part intensely about yourself and love, now is the time to profoundly change your limiting behavioral patterns about relationships. Because these patterns usually arise early, sometimes even during pregnancy or even earlier, it is important to use an exercise that starts before the pattern was created. You have already done this exercise in the part "Quantum Energy and Health." It is about the immensely powerful exercise "transformation of cell consciousness." You will be able to completely change your cell information and even create a new past. The exciting thing about this exercise is that you can relive your negative experiences from the past but in a totally new way. More on that later.

As mentioned in the last part, I would like to recommend to not read the exercise and then perform it. It's just too intense to memorize it. Record it on your cell phone, or have an individual with meditation experience read the exercise out loud.

You can also order the CD "Transformation of Cell Consciousness II—Finally Feeling Love Again" at my online shop or Amazon.

Are you ready for a new attitude toward life? Then find a quiet place where you can be undisturbed for the next twenty minutes. Have a pen and notepad ready.

TRANSFORMATION OF CELL CONSCIOUSNESS—FINALLY FEELING LOVE AGAIN

As always, take the kinesiological test to see if now is the right and appropriate time to work on the pattern that you want to let go of.[44]

If your body has agreed to the exercise, go one step further: Ask yourself what your "instead" is, the instead of the old pattern. Make sure that your "instead" has something to do with you. "I want to be loved" would be a less recommendable phrase because it would change only your outside. More appropriate would be "I am worthy of being loved" or "I experience perfect love." Perfect would be "I love myself and through it I radiate love."

What is your "instead"? Name it and write it down on your notepad.

Do you remember one situation in your life in which you already felt this "instead," even if it was only for a brief moment? Then close your eyes and go back in your memory to the point where you felt it. Experience this moment again with all your senses.

Do not look at it like it's a movie, but instead be in the situation. Relive the situation again.

Just like back then when you felt how wonderful it was, go in it all the way. The moment the feeling is the strongest, place your left or right hand on your heart, and anchor that feeling into this movement. After a few seconds, take your hand off your heart, and come back to the now consciousness. Open your eyes.

---

[44] You can find more information on the subject of kinesiology on page 36.

How was it to experience this wonderful feeling again? Now get up and do something different for a moment that has nothing to do with this exercise. Then sit or lie down again. Focus on anything that comes to mind. Now test your anchor. Place your hand on your heart just like you did during the exercise. Can you feel that beautiful feeling immediately? If this is not the case, repeat the exercise, and place your anchor until the anchor is set. It should work with the second try.

That was the first part of the exercise. Now let's go on a journey through your life. Close your eyes again. Your hands lay completely quiet on or next to your body but not on your heart. Notice your breath as it comes and goes. Your entire focus is on your breath. Inhale three times deeply. Feel the oxygen filling up your lungs, how your chest and your stomach rise and fall. When inhaling, think *I breathe in love, security, and protection*, and when exhaling, *I exhale all negative energy from my cells*. Notice how your body relaxes more with every breath you take.

Now let your entire life go backward in your mind. This usually happens very quickly, and you will encounter situations in which you recognize your old behavioral patterns (e.g., of not being loved or being an outsider or where you had to fully surrender). Imagine placing a marker at this point on the timeline of your life as if you would place a needle on a map. Place an *X* at this point in your life. Go through your entire adulthood, go back to your young adulthood, to youth, to your childhood, to early childhood, all the way back to your birth. You will recognize certain situations that you will mark. Then experience your birth. Go further back to the time when you grew in your mother's womb, as a fetus and then as an embryo, back to the time of your conception. Notice your procreation and then go back further. Now you are just a soul. This is where you stop. Enjoy the time as a soul in which you are completely free. Here is perfect, unconditional love. Here is all the knowledge of the universe, absolute peace and quiet, perfection in its purest form. Now you can feel all of it. The connection to all souls in the universe, the oneness with everything and with God.

Even if you want to stay here forever, remember that you are coming back to earth so you can gain more experiences. Prepare yourself for your life. Go to the room of visions. Here you will meet many souls. All of them will accompany you on the path of your life. They will be your friends, casual acquaintances, teachers, and many more. Some souls are particularly courageous because they make themselves available to you by triggering and creating conflicts and arguments. These souls are so loving that they will offer themselves as a mirror to you, showing you your deepest issues. You should thank them now, because later, as an earth child, you will perceive them as anything other than loving.

But that's exactly what they are: a mirror to yourself.

Now look at your own birth vision, just as you imagined life, in every detail, to get exactly the experience you want to have. Recognize that you had to have the opposite experiences of this—only to realize later how important it was to experience all of it. Now meet your future parents, and recognize what you will learn from them. See your friends, your partners, and all the other important people in your life. Recognize all your imprints that will determine your life, all the good and bad experiences. They are all the ultimate and important experiences you had to make. Every step is right. This is your ideal life's course. Recognize that you will often deviate from the ideal path. And that's a good thing too. Take a close look at everything—your potentials, talents, preferences, passions, gifts, and destiny.

Now leave the room of visions and say goodbye to the souls. Now decide on your new life, and feel how that decision creates a new vibration that goes to earth and is already placing the first imprint.

Recall the feeling of your "instead" by placing your hand on your heart. Feel what you want instead, and get ready to immerse yourself in your life. Release your hand from your heart. Are you ready to relive your life but now with the feeling of being loved, wanted, and accepted? Whatever your "instead," is, it's now finding its way into your life.

QUANTUM ENERGY AND RELATIONSHIPS

Now watch your parents melted together and about to father a child: you!

Feel the love that connects the two that your parents are experiencing. Recognize how the egg and sperm cells merge with each other and all the love that flows within. These cells already contain perfect love and trust and the excitement for life. Recognize how the first cell division begins and how more love grows and is getting bigger and bigger with each cell division. Every single cell is flooded with love. You develop into an embryo, becoming a fetus. Arms and legs and all organs develop. If your old pattern emerged in this stage, replace it with your new feeling. Should you need your anchor here, place your hand on your heart. Your cell information is transforming. You are growing in your mother's womb and feeling how life force is getting bigger and bigger. You are looking forward to being born soon. Then the time has come: the birth! You are screaming out loud and looking forward to life. Look into the smiling faces of your parents and the midwife. They are all so happy to see you. Experience the first few days as a baby, then your early childhood. Do you find markers here that you have set in advance that show your old patterns? Then replace the new feeling with the old one. If necessary, release your anchor. Notice that you experience all situations in a completely new way. Your memories change too. Your cellular consciousness is transforming; you override your DNA. You experience your childhood completely new, although the situations remain the same.

You grow up from child to adolescent. All markers are replaced, all situations are relived, the cell information changes.

Feel how your strength, self-confidence, self-worth, and love grows stronger and stronger. You are grown up now and getting closer and closer to the present. At some point, you arrive in today. But let life flow into your future. Notice how you get older and experience a wonderful future. You are enjoying your future to the fullest. You love life. Just before you arrive on the day where your soul would leave your body and the body dies, you stop. Look at your last day, the day you died. Feel now that death is something completely natural. You were born to die someday. Die and become is part of creation. Death means shedding your body so the soul can slip into a new body a short time after. The soul never dies. Happy and fulfilled, you are looking forward to the moment of death because you know that you have achieved everything.

Now turn around and look back to the present. What did you experience? What have you done in love? How did you live? How did you experience your parents and your children? How did love change your life? Who was with you? What special situations have influenced your life? What did you do with it? Take a close look at your timeline. Do you recognize how your new behavioral patterns have completely renewed your cellular consciousness? Wonderful! Thank yourself for the life that you have created—a life of love and wonderful relationships.

Now you are traveling back to the present. Once there, you will be aware of your body. Feel yourself sitting in your chair or laying on your sofa. Focus on your breath as it comes and goes.

Take three deep breaths again to fully arrive in your now consciousness. When the time is right for you, open your eyes. Arrive in the here and now. Take a notepad and write down your thoughts and experiences.

Enjoy the moment and the time to come. You may have felt a lot during the exercise. Wait and see what is about to change.

Due to many inquiries, I have developed a resolution for birth trauma with a special transformation of cell consciousness. Should you be affected, I highly recommend the CD to you.[45]

---

[45] You can order the CD "Transformation of Cell Consciousness V—Birth Traumas" and all other CDs at Amazon or my online shops, www.quantumenergycoaching.com.

THE RELATIONSHIP WITH YOUR PARTNER

> "In hope of being loved by another, the tender bud of love for itself withers."

What does "partnership" mean to you? What are your expectations on your significant other? "Excuse me?" you may ask. "Shouldn't I have any expectations!" Yes, that's right, it would be perfect if you could free yourself from any expectations. But, honestly, are there not a few expectations? How should your partner be? What's important to you in a relationship? Is it, first and foremost, about having someone on your side and to be loved?

Is it about "getting" something that you are missing? Do you want to give love?

Become aware of your answers to these questions to find out what expectations you have in a partnership. Can your significant other meet them?

Often we want our partner to fulfill them, but we should do that for ourselves first. And here we are, right back at the centerpiece of relationships—ourselves!

THE ROLE OF THE PARTNER IN YOUR THEATER OF LIFE

*"The relationship with the partner is the mirror,
in which we recognize ourselves."*

Do you want your partner to be loving? Then ask yourself how loving you are to yourself. Should he/she finally get moving and taking life into their own hands? Then ask yourself where you cannot get going. Do you think that he/she doesn't pay enough attention to you? Then ask yourself where you hardly pay any attention to yourself.

Your partner fulfills additional tasks in your relationship that you consciously recognize but also tasks that you do not consciously acknowledge.

- They are a platform for things you don't want.
- They are a mirror to you for what you cannot recognize in yourself.
- They show you your deepest issues.

Your protective ego will certainly not like these statements, but your partner—besides your children—are the best way to get to know yourself.

THE PROJECTION

Do you remember the question from your childhood "When you point your finger at someone, how many fingers point back at you?"

This is exactly what it's all about. If you don't like something about your partner, then you subconsciously project something you don't like about yourself onto him/her. I bet your ego is telling you now that this isn't it at all. Of course not, because you don't want to see it in yourself either. That's why you need your significant other to point it out.

In all the judgments you make about your partner, you can always ask yourself: "What does this have to do with me?" If you are honest with yourself about it, you will recognize that this is also part of you, what you noticed in your partner. Just imagine what it would be like if you could say, "Okay, so am I." That's the big goal that you can accept yourself the way you are. You may get annoyed for being like that, or you can accept it. The fact is you are like that! But now that you have recognized it within yourself, you can change it. Before then, you only saw it in your partner.

All of this not only applies to your partner but also to other people. The more you learn letting go of judgments and ratings in your life, the freer you will become—to yourself and toward others. Imagine you could accept everyone as they are. How simple and easy life would be—pure joy! This too is a wisdom of quantum consciousness: if the judgments fall, the vibration will no longer find a negative resonance within others.

THE MIRROR

This law goes one step further. Your partner also reflects behavior that you cannot recognize within yourself because it is still dormant in your subconscious. Your significant other also brings out some things in you. Not always pretty, but true. Instead of judging your partner, you should be grateful to him/her for providing themselves as a mirror to you.

Why is it that you are reflecting yourself in the other person? In biology, we speak of the so-called mirror neurons, which we have within us. These ensure that we can empathize with other people, for example. We feel what others feel. In the same way, the mirror neurons ensure that we are recognizing aspects of ourselves in the other person.[46]

This also eliminates the question of fault. If your partner is only the "project platform" or the mirror for you, then they are not to blame.

I also would like to mention: the principle of personal responsibility is one of the most important in quantum consciousness. There is nobody else to blame if you take full responsibility for your life. Neither are you to blame for anything that happens to others unless you contribute purposely to it. If you change your point of view, the question of blame does not come up anymore.

The question of fault is eliminated when we recognize that our partner is just a 'project platform' or our mirror

---

[46] More about the subject mirror neurons in the book by Joachim Bauer *Why I Feel What You Feel* (Heyne Publisher, 2006).

QUANTUM ENERGY AND RELATIONSHIPS

So if your significant other pushes your buttons, it can only happen if their behavior resonated within you. If there is a response, it must have something to do with you too, otherwise it wouldn't resonate. In quantum mechanics, two particles only enter with resonance to each other when they are in proximity and connected to each other. Your partner's behavior reminds you unconsciously of a family member (e.g., your father, mother, uncle, etc.).

Take this opportunity to find out exactly what it is that is upsetting you. Be curious, and do not "stomp" on the opposite person. Don't justify yourself for things that don't need justification.

Now do the following exercise.

STOP, CHALLENGE, CHOOSE

As soon as you realize that your partner presses one of your buttons, pause for a moment, then take a step back, either literally or in your mind. This will decrease the emotion. Consciously breathe in several times through your heart and out through your solar plexus. You will automatically become calmer. Your focus changes. Then go actively into source consciousness, the "gap" between the thoughts. Then feel within yourself: What pain came up in this moment through the behavior or statement made by your counterpart? Explore yourself. How would you normally react in this moment? And why? With what aim or to what effect? Make a new decision for yourself now, and react differently than you used to. Surprise your significant other with this new reaction, and use the opportunity to talk to your partner about your "buttons." Get to know and understand each other better.

If you do this exercise repeatedly, you will eventually become an expert in yourself and will enjoy lightening up your "buttons." In this moment, the negative emotions loosen their strength and will change permanently

Stop-Challenge-Choose

Retrieve-Questioning-Decision

↓

**The decision is yours!
Decide for yourself
how you manage your emotional state
and thus control your results.**

Counteract to your typical behavior

THE DEEPEST ISSUES

If your partner shows you one of your deepest issues, they are doing you a special service of love. Of course, it will be one of your issues which you find difficult to accept. Your issue is a distant aspect of yourself. I would like to tell you a short story about this.

Two years ago, my partner at the time decided to see a therapist because of our deadlocked relationship. And, because a relationship always involves both sides, the therapist suggested that she brings me along. At first I made excuses but later thought to myself, *Well, I'll go with her* without knowing what I would get myself into. So I found myself in the middle of an intensive therapy session, although in the past I had always thought that "something like that" was only for other people. Looking back today, I was glad that I was attending those meetings.

The therapist was extremely attentive and able to recognize things that were very subtle. I talked about different situations. Suddenly she caught me talking about something with a smug smile on my face, which was mean. If someone else would have made me aware of it, I would never have believed that I could talk so enthusiastically about mean things. She, however, revealed it, and I realized what I had just done. My unconscious role which I lived all my life, being the lovely, nice neighbor.

I would never have agreed that I could be mean too.

Why? Quite simple—it would have called my role into question.

The therapist uncovered a dark side of me which I kept securely hidden and only came to light when it was hardly noticeable. I hurt others very subtle in these moments. Looking back, I noticed a few other mean behaviors in me. Today I know that it was my way of letting all my frustrations out that I've accumulated all my life. Because of my need for harmony, I never gave my anger free range. After I understood why I did it, I learned to accept my deep issues. Subsequently, that side of me faded.

My current partner relationship has now lasted three and a half years, and I have shown my dark side once—with the result that my wife was very hurt. Do I need that? Obviously I did in the past, but no longer today. However, I have realized and accepted that my deepest issues are a part of me. As a result, this part finds more and more peace and hasn't appeared. It was important to own up to my deepest issues but also to be honest with myself about it, which allowed me to be honest with my wife. Again, it shows how important it is to be honest with your partner.

Deep-rooted issues in yourself are considered bad and have been buried safely, wrapped around with a pink ribbon on it. For most people, it is extremely difficult to recognize them. However, you notice them in your partner. How does this work? Ask yourself the following question:

What is it about your partner (your parents, your child, your boss, etc.) that you dislike the most?

I am correct in assuming that you will have an answer ready immediately. Congratulations, here is one of your own deepest issues. You don't want to admit it? I can understand that, and yet it is the truth. Now there are two options: First, you argue about it and continue to reject it. What will happen? The energy follows the attention, and so the dark side seeks more moments where it can live it out. Secondly, you deal with this part of you until you understand and accept it lovingly. It will pacify this aspect over time and will no longer need attention.

Another aspect of deep issues is distortion. If you have received many orders, and prohibitions were imposed on you to constantly behave well ("child, sit straight at the table," "eat with a knife and fork," "eat slowly," "don't do that," etc.), then you have built yourself an artificial world of good manners. However, they do not teach what real kindness and helpfulness means. Later, natural behavior appears in a distorted form (e.g., as greed, overcorrectness, or exuberant politeness). The extreme form is borderline syndrome, in which a person lives two lives—the life of the normal and the split-off part.

If you learned as a toddler that nudity is not good, you will judge situations later related to it (e.g., nudism) and classify them as sin. Were you caught masturbating as a child? You received a harsh punishment for it? That too becomes a sin. Later, the results are often having a troubled relationship with your own body and sexuality.

A deep issue can also be associated with a good act and an unpleasant situation. For example, when you were a toddler and played loudly with joy while your grandmother was laying sick in the bed and you were told by your parents, "When you are so loud playing, Grandma will stay sick," this too shapes you as a child. At this early stage, you believe that when you play loudly, it makes others sick. If Grandma dies shortly after, it may well be that you feel responsible for it. At this age, you cannot consciously separate the situation and your behavior. Later, you condemn loud children without knowing why and become a quiet and reserved person. Exuberance is taboo, and joy is only allowed if other people are feeling well. The patterns that you have developed in childhood can be found and have manifested in many variations. They are often so tricky that they require a close examination. In such a case, you need a professional that is specialized with these subjects. To recognize one's own deep issues and to accept them in love is extremely challenging for most people.

These are exactly the aspects that you strongly judge in your partner or in another person. However, if you have uncovered through the question "What is it that I dislike about my partner?" (my parents, my child, my boss, etc.), if you have found out what one or more of your deepest issues are and where they come from, you can use the following exercise to help you to easily accept them.

ACCEPT YOUR OWN ISSUES WITH LOVE

Find a quiet place, a chair, or lie on the couch. Give full attention to the energy center of your heart, which is in the center of your rib cage.[47] Place your left hand on this point for support, the other hand on another body part that you prefer. Say the following sentence in your mind: "I accept my deepest issues with love," and go into source consciousness. Linger there for at least thirty seconds, and enjoy the moment. Then release the hand positions, and come back to your now consciousness.

Repeat the exercise as often as you like. Over time you can leave your hands off. They only serve as support.

When you are ready to lovingly accept your deepest issues, you will bring back the split-off part into your life and will become whole again. The nice thing about it is that there is an immense amount of power that will strengthen yourself.[48]

---

[47] Also known as the heart chakra.
[48] So far, there is little literature on working with one's own deep-rooted issues. I recommend two books by Debbie Ford: *The Dark Side of the Light Chasers* (Goldmann, 1999) and *The Shadow Effect* (Kamphausen, 2011).

GET RID OF FEARS AND BELIEFS

"Change your beliefs and you will change your life."

I talked in detail about the subject fear. So I just want to mention it here briefly. What does fear have to do with a partner relationship? Take a close look at your fears. What hidden beliefs could be the reasons? For example, if you are afraid that your partner doesn't really love you, you may have an unconscious belief that "I'm not worthy being loved." Are you afraid that your partner will leave you? Have you felt like this often, and are you extremely jealous? Could it be that there is a hidden belief like "I am not lovable, therefore people abandoned me"?

Remember the life's model.[49] A belief, whether consciously or unconsciously, insures that exactly that repeatedly happens in your life. Until you change your beliefs. Explore the beliefs about your relationship fears. Get to know yourself a little better. You will find out the root of this belief. Chances are you'll find it in your early childhood.

Once you have found out what your beliefs are and how they affect your life, you can begin to change those beliefs. Always do the exercise "making contact" first to find out what your belief would like to make you aware of, and use the already-introduced changing beliefs exercise. Relationship fears can also be reduced.

If this is not the case, apply the exercise "freeing yourself from fears."

---

[49] See pages 47 to 58.

LOOKING FOR YOUR DREAM PARTNER

> "We have been looking for our dream partner for a lifetime. In all this time, we've met them hundreds of times without even recognizing it."

I hate to destroy dreams, but, for many, the search for the dream partner will remain an eternal search. We have extremely high demands on our dream partner. Hardly anyone can live up to them. There are people waiting a lifetime for their prince or their supermodel and therefore find themselves in many new unsatisfying relationships. The paradox is, due to your high standards, you have probably already walked past the dream partner many times. Your focus was clearly on the ideal type that you walked through life with blinders on.

For example, in terms of the idol of beauty, my dream partner was a Brazilian woman. That was until I met several Brazilian women. The idol of beauty was fulfilled, but their character wasn't what I was looking for at all. It may be that there is a Brazilian woman that has my ideal character, but what do you think the chances are that I will meet exactly that person?

Today I recognize my dream partner in my wife. She is not Brazilian, but she offers everything I wanted. That was only possible by saying goodbye to my idol. I let go and stopped looking. I closed one door, and another opened. Behind it was something much more beautiful. I could only recognize that after I opened the new door.

Letting go means closing a door behind you so that you can open a new one.

I would like to share one more secret with you at this point. Would your dream partner ever have a chance to step into your life if he/she would exist? Take this test. Stand in front of the mirror, and ask yourself how beautiful and ideal you find yourself. Can you say with all your heart that you are a dream person? I bet you just realize the secret for yourself. When you don't feel that you are the ideal type, how should the prince or princess ever find you? Only when and if you fully accept and love yourself for who you are can you send the right vibrational frequency to the person of your dreams.

You may have been in the relationship with your dream partner for a while without even knowing it. If you let go of all the judgments you have against your current significant other and accept them and not criticize them, you may see their potential of being your dream partner. Isn't that amazing? You don't have to go out into the world and search for them. They have been here all along. Behind everything you don't like about them is the most beautiful and best person there is. Why else would you have chosen them to begin with?

Clearly not because you have been drunk or haven't cleaned your glasses. Most likely not. Recognize the person that you have originally fallen for. Start by talking to each other. Be honest, and don't blame or judge one another. Talk about your feelings in the relationship, and start taking a good look at yourself. It may take time for your partner to join in. Yet when you realize that your significant other is only your "project platform," or your mirror, or the one in which you realize your own deepest issues, if you can look past that, then you will realize they are still the one who they were at the beginning of your relationship. They are even greater than that because they assist you in working through your own issues. The infatuation phase only lasts for a moment no matter what. A dream relationship is one in which both grow by pressing each other's buttons. Such a relationship needs a lot of openness and honesty—toward oneself and toward the other—mindfulness, and communication.

QUANTUM ENERGY AND RELATIONSHIPS

Furthermore, I would like to introduce you to an exercise that can be a cornerstone for an amazing dream relationship.[50]

The ten-minute exercise so that it doesn't have to happen anymore.

---

[50] I would like to thank my former partner for introducing me to this exercise in ours past relationship. She made it possible for me to express my deepest feelings and fears.

TEN MINUTES FOR AN HONEST RELATIONSHIP

Make an agreement with your partner. Everything you will communicate to them is only intended to express your feelings. Everything can be said without using it against you later. This agreement is important because only that way can honest communication be possible.

Sit across from each other. You each have ten minutes to talk about your feelings and how you are doing in the relationship while the other only listens. It is important for the one who speaks to only talk about their own feelings. Every accusation, judgment, or evaluation is counterproductive. Speak only about yourself. Of course, you can mention situations which were not okay from your point of view. Tell them what it did to you, and not what they did wrong.

For example, "It seems to me that you forgot our anniversary. It hurts me, and I feel like this because this day is especially important to me" or "I feel in our relationship emotionally underserved. We cuddle a little with each other, but an intimate relationship is especially important to me. However, caring for each other and lying together is especially important." "I wish…" You don't have to look at your partner when speaking. It helped me a lot the first time looking down because I could better connect to my emotional level. After ten minutes, switch roles.

Be sure to stick to the ten-minute limit. Don't go over, or don't do less than that. If you feel you are done after five minutes, dig a little deeper. Wait and see what else is coming up. Sometimes it takes time for issues to became known that were previously hidden, or, if you were afraid, it may boomerang if you would bring them up.

The more you do this exercise, especially keeping your agreement, the more you will learn about yourself and each other. When you are ready, you can increase your time to fifteen minutes. Often we don't address aspects of the relationship out of frustration or fear of the boomerang effect because the partner immediately will counter or justify themselves. This exercise has helped many relationships to heal. You will learn to be honest in your relationship and to talk about yourself.

THE RELATIONSHIP WITH YOUR PARENTS

"Always remember: You have chosen your parents!"

Your parents are the people who have shaped your life the most. As already described in the second part, children are unable to consciously respond until the age of six because their brain is not yet able to build consciousness. So the child unconsciously absorbs everything. Everything Mom or Dad says and what they do and how they react, the child perceives as right and true. What our parents tell us about ourselves, we become. In the first few days and weeks after birth, the baby only focuses on the eyes and face of the parents. Glowing eyes on Mom and Dad's smiling faces are the reference the child takes in that everything is fine. Later, the child places everything it does in reference to that expression. It learns very quickly what is good and what is not so good even without the parents saying anything. When the parents are there, the child feels loved and accepted. If it has been separated from the mother after birth, because the baby was premature or due to complications, the child is missing the necessary love and closeness it had for nine months in the womb. Later as an adult, he or she will, most likely, compensate this lack of closeness and will subconsciously choose partners who will offer less closeness. A paradox like so many in our lives.

QUANTUM ENERGY AND RELATIONSHIPS

The baby focused on Mom's eyes.

For the baby, parents are the reference for all that is good. Consequently, it tries to imitate everything Mom or Dad does because it believes all of this is correct. In this early stage, the baby already takes over behavioral patterns of the parents. This is one of the reasons why you are, as an adult, like your mother or father, even if you don't want to admit it. That's another reason you often subconsciously seek partners who are like your parents. I know you don't want to hear that either. Honestly, have you thought to yourself before, *Now he/she is exactly like my mother/father*? This is completely normal, because you have learned that the behavior of Mom and Dad is the best in the world. So that's what you want—of course unconsciously—from your significant other.

RECOGNIZE A PART OF YOUR PARENTS IN YOURSELF

Have a pen and notepad ready. Explore yourself. Which behavior do you recognize within yourself that you have learned from your parents? What beliefs, attitudes, and values are those that you still hear about today or heard back then? Listen carefully to yourself, and write down what you've discovered. You will find that the list can get quite long.

Dig a little deeper, and look at all aspects you may live today that your parents wanted from you back then because they could not live it themselves. Your correctness, your pursuit of perfection, your career, your hobbies, your current occupation, your style of dress, etc. Parents often unconsciously transfer dreams that they could not live out onto their children. Write all of it down on your list.

You will need this list for the next exercise.

Take another look at your list. All of these are aspects that are not yours. Now is the time to give them back to where they belong: to your parents. Are you ready for it? Then prepare yourself for an intense meditation. Let's clean the slate and create a balance of energy. You will give everything back to your parents what belongs to them. Furthermore, you can tell them everything you always wanted to tell them but never had the courage to do so for whatever reason. You can say all that needs to be said. You need to be also willing to receive the same from your parents. For both sides, there is some cleaning up to do.

You will notice, even if you do this all in your imagination, your relationship with your parents will change a lot—even if they have already passed. Record this exercise via cell phone, or acquire the corresponding CD for the book so that you can get the most out of the exercise.[51]

---

[51] The CD is finally free! The USA version and Cd's will be available at www.QuantumEnergyCoaching.com

THE PARENT PROCESS

Take about thirty minutes for this meditation. As always, choose a quiet place where you will not be disturbed. Look at your list again from the previous exercise, and read the aspects of your parents that you have recognized within yourself. Then set the notes aside.

Make yourself as comfortable as possible. Sit on a chair, then place your feet next to each other on the floor, and make sure that your legs are not crossed. That way, chi, your life energy, can flow evenly. Should you prefer lying down, have your legs next to each other, and rest your arms beside your body. Close your eyes, and concentrate on your breath. Take three deep breaths, and feel how you take in new energy when inhaling and how you blow out used energy when exhaling. With every breath you take, you can feel how you relax more. Now imagine that you are standing in an elevator and going down ten floors. With every floor that you leave behind, you sink deeper into relaxation. Once you arrive on the main floor, you are very calm and relaxed. Recognize how completely calm and relaxed you are. Enjoy this moment of absolute silence.

Now get ready for your trip. Imagine how you travel to a wonderful place. This can be a place you already know or a place that you create in your imagination. When you arrive there, take a close look: What do you see, what do you hear, how do you feel here? Are you all right? Now look around, and find a place where you can make yourself comfortable. That could be under a tree, on the beach, anywhere. Make sure that you have peace and quiet and that you are alone. Again, enjoy being alone. Now invite your father to join you and recognize seeing him in the distance walking toward you. He is getting closer and closer. You see him smiling, approaching you. Now invite him to sit in front of you. Tell him why you invited him. Today is the day you will speak honestly with each other. Tell him that there are things you are going to tell him now that need to be said.

He will sit there and just listen without interrupting you.

Now is your turn. Let your father know what you have to say to him. Let him know, and don't leave anything out. All those things that you have never dared saying before. If you can, tell him in love. You can also express your anger, frustration, and sadness freely. Try to keep your anger to yourself, if you can, because it's your anger. Take all the time you need.

Finally, feel inside yourself whether everything was said. Then give him back all the aspects that are his that you have on your list. Place the aspects symbolically in front of him so that he can take it back. Did you give everything back? Feel within yourself whether there is anything else you would like to share or return.

When you're done, switch roles. Now it's your father's turn to communicate. Just listen to his words. Let the little boy or girl inside yourself listen too. Much is meant for your inner child. Just listen. Take and receive the aspects that your father wants to give you back that originally belonged to you. Take the aspects and feel how pieces are restored within you. Healing is allowed to happen. When your father said it all and gave you everything back, end his conversation with an act of forgiveness. Place your hand on his heart, and say, "I forgive you." Then place your hand on your heart and say: "I forgive myself." Feel the act of forgiveness. Now your father is performing the forgiveness ritual. Feel again what happens inside of you when your father forgives you. Finally, hug each other. Maybe do it like you've never done it before in your life. Feel the love between you and your father. Let the love flow and merge with each other. Thank your father for sharing all of this with you, and say goodbye to him. Let him go.

Now invite your mother over, and do the same exercise with her. Don't leave anything out, and end the meeting with your mother with the act of forgiveness. Give her a big hug and thank her. Now let your mother leave. Stay at your place for a while longer. Feel what has changed, how you have become whole again, how healing was allowed to happen. When it feels right, prepare yourself to return from your journey. Look back one more time, enjoy the view, and return from your journey with a completely new attitude toward life.

Go back into the elevator. With every floor ascending, you come back more to your now awareness. Once arrived at the tenth floor, you get out. Recognize your surroundings. Feel yourself sitting in your chair or laying on your sofa or bed. Feel yourself completely in the present. Feel your arms, your legs, your entire body. Take three deep breaths. After the third breath, you are consciously in the here and now—with this new attitude toward life, a new freedom, wholeness. Stretch yourself. Open your eyes, and thank yourself for what you just have accomplished.

Feel within yourself. What has changed? Think about your father, then about your mother. Have the feelings changed toward them? Enjoy this new feeling. Write down what you've just experienced.

You can also do this exercise with your grandparents or siblings. In any case, healing can take place.

At this point, I would like to repeat the act of forgiveness. Of course, you can do this exercise with any person or toward an animal that you have a conflict with, no matter how old that conflict is. Forgiveness always works beyond time.

Performing the forgiveness ritual independently of the parenting process will further expand it.

THE FORGIVENESS RITUAL

Imagine that the person or animal you want to forgive is standing right in front of you. Place your hand on their heart and say "I forgive you." Place your hand on your own heart and say "I forgive myself." Now take your hand from your heart and imagine how to bundle the old energy of conflict by clenching your hand into a fist. Now throw away this energy, and speak out loud: "And I let go." By throwing away the old energy, you will release it from your body's system. Do not do the action mechanically, but feel the forgiveness deep down from your heart. Healing can happen.

The three steps:

1. I forgive you.
2. I forgive myself.
3. And I let go.[52]

Can you imagine that your parents showed you the greatest love they had? Do you believe that they have done everything in their power to give you what you needed for your life? Once you have put aside all the hurt and resentment, then you may be able to feel all of this. Often your parents didn't know any better and passed on to you what they have learned from their parents. After the parenting process and forgiveness exercise, you can recognize and perceive and feel the love from your parents. Now you can acknowledge and accept this love. Always remember: your parents did the best they could—in their own way.

---

[52] I thank my wife, Sonja, for this very touching exercise.

I wish you could get to a point where you can make peace with your mother and father and that remaining wounds are allowed to heal. It took me a long time to forgive my mother from the bottom of my heart, and I was able to tell her that I loved her despite all the pain and resentment that was within me. Yet you can imagine what these three words meant for my mother at that moment. That I could tell her that she did everything right. Often mothers and fathers think that they did everything wrong in their parenting. A huge burden can be released when they hear out of their child's mouth that all was done correctly. You can't change what happened, but you can change your relationship and your feelings about it today.

The Power of Forgiveness

In the last few days, I've realized how much I have changed. Considering that I couldn't exchange three sentences with my mother without accusing and arguing, I now have spent one of my best days with her during the last holiday. We laughed a lot, did outside activities, and the kids enjoyed it too. When I returned home with my children late that day, my heart was overjoyed, and I had a satisfying smile on my face. All was simply perfect. I have become much more relaxed; taking my chil-

dren also as role models and deviated away from my straight-line-nonsense parenting. I enjoy being in the world and having great people by my side. What an abundance!

(Seran Ok, Sins, Switzerland)

THE RELATIONSHIP WITH YOUR CHILDREN

> "If we were able to look through the eyes of
> a child, we would see a new world."

Your children are the most honest mirrors you can have. They reflect your life in their childlike way back to you. As a result, these mirrors often feel more intense than of adults. I made this painful experience myself in my past relationship. My previous partner had one six-year-old son. In this age, children constantly test their limits. As an outsider, I could see well how the son lived the negative patterns of the mother, which made her upset. I was not spared either. It was a great challenge for me too, while I was not prepared for the task.

For example, the child always needed attention when my partner and I had an important conversation. Prior, he could have played by himself, and suddenly, he was sitting with us and wanted to be entertained. Back then, it really got my adrenaline pumping. Later, when I reflected on the situation, I realized that both of us—each in our own way—longed for the attention of the "woman in the house." This little man pushed my buttons with great force so that my recognition pattern was in full swing.

Situations like this happen all day long between parents and children. Unfortunately, we find it difficult to deal with it in the moment when emotions are running high. It is more important to reflect in retrospect what exactly our children are unconsciously pointing out to us.

REFLECTION OF RESONANCE THROUGH YOUR CHILD

Write down where and how you react to your child and what you do to make it resonate with you. Explore yourself and your patterns regarding your child. What did you discover? What does your child reflect in you? Learn to understand why your child is creating this resonance in you. When you understand it, use the various exercises from this or the previous part to help you to transform your old beliefs and behavioral patterns from your childhood.

Thank your child for making you aware of your own issues.

You may be brave enough to go a step further. Take your children as a role model because they still do everything from their childlikeness. They live their birth right of free will we have so diligently weaned ourselves off as adults. They are much freer from rules and guidelines, moral aspects, and judgments. We still can learn a lot from children.

Many people ask me what the optimal upbringing should look like. This book cannot be a parenting educational guide, and I'm not a parental expert either. Still, I want to give you some pointers that I learned myself through the new sciences:

As a mother, make sure that your child is placed immediately after birth on your chest and that it can stay there for a while. In the following days, your child should be placed on your chest as well. For the child, the birth is an infinitely great shock, because its security was taken away and it was suddenly separated from the source to which it was just recently bound. However, if it's placed close to its mother's heart afterward, the baby will feel the connection again in an instant. Love continues to flow directly and noticeably. This heart connection can lead to the child being peaceful and sociable, crying less and sleeping better.

Furthermore, I would like to recommend that you parent your child consciously. If you give them your love and attention, encourage them, and demand and only set limits where it is necessary, then your child can develop completely naturally—according to his/her gifts and potentials. Encourage what your child is good at, and do not work on eliminating the weaknesses—strengthen strengths instead of compensating for weaknesses. The energy expenditure is much higher in the weaknesses, and it is a lot of stress for the child.

I've learned to go with the flow, not forcefully creating changes. In the first three years of a child's life, it is in the phase of self-identity. It soaks up everything around it. Use this super-learning phase by teaching them lots of things. For example, during this time, children can learn three different languages.

If the child is overwhelmed, it will let you know quickly by losing the attention and turning away from it. I know this recommendation is in, today's world, a great challenge, but your child will thank you a thousandfold for your efforts.

Why do you think a child is rampaging or doing nonsense? It tries in its own way to get attention because it learned that it doesn't get it the regular way. However, in our busy world today, we get stressed out easily by running from appointment to appointment and having a thousand other things on our mind we often miss the first tender call for attention.

In my workshops, I like to tell the following story about it: Two mothers standing in the front yard and talk very animatedly. The subject is extremely exciting. Little Lena, one year old, would like to be held by her mother. She is standing close to her mother's leg and lifts her arms up to symbolize that she would like to be held. Nothing happens because the mother is fixated on the conversation. Lena tugs at her mother's pants, but she doesn't react because she doesn't notice. After a while, little Lena cries, but still the mother does not react.

At some point, Lena starts screaming because she can't speak yet. Finally, she gets her mother's attention. She looks incredibly angry and asks what the matter is. The child lifts her arms up again and is now picked up by her mother. What do you think will happen when this situation repeats a few times?

Little Lena learns that she gets attention when she screams.

In the future, she won't try to put her arms up but will scream immediately. The result of this is that the mother often gets annoyed and wonders why the child is screaming so often.

The unconscious desire for attention

Little Luke has a different experience. He's already two years old. Instead of complaining, he kicks his mother in the leg. The mother, incredibly angry, cannot understand why Luke is doing this and punishes him. Luke also learns that he gets attention when he's behaving badly. So he will do that repeatedly in the future. But Lena and Luke learn something else too. They learn that it is not good to want attention because they have been punished for it or received an evil look. You can imagine what that means for the future of Lena and Luke and how they will outlive their behavioral patterns. Living a life and constantly seeking attention and having the most intelligent strategies to do so.

At the same time, creating situations for themselves that ensure that they are getting punished.

How can you support your child now when they have already developed these patterns? Do the opposite of what you have been doing so far. Don't punish your child. Hold them in the arms. Do it repeatedly. At some point, the child realizes that it no longer needs to act out to attract your attention. Feed your child with love as often as you can. Feel the love you have for your child, because this is how you nourish yourself at the same time and even heal your own issues.

Many mothers are annoyed that the father is parenting the child completely different. His job is not to nourish and emotionally support. His job is to prepare the child for the "world out there" and to give them courage for the things the mother is so diligently trying to protect them from.

I have a single parent in my immediate environment who tries to shield her child from everything. Naturally, this is correct because that is her job. Yet, at some point, the child will get its difficulties in the "hard, rough world." To prepare it would have been the father's responsibility. He loosened the reins which the mother kept firm. Both are correct, and that is immensely important. (If you are a single parent, I recommend you loosen up now and then so your child can have the experiences it needs to have—even if your protective instinct begins to rebel.)

FROM THE ALLEGED DISEASE ADHD

"Today's children are way ahead of us."

You are wondering why I am talking about ADHD and why ADHD was not included in the "Quantum Energy and Health" part. It's simple: for me, hyperactivity has absolutely nothing to do with an "illness." For me, ADHD clearly belongs in this area "Relationships with Our Children" (more on that later).

Relevant lexicons describe attention-deficit hyperactivity disorder, or ADHD for short, as a mental disorder that is already in the onset of early childhood and is characterized by difficulties with attention, impulsiveness, and hyperactivity. About 3 to 10 percent of all children show symptoms like ADHD. If that is so, our society would have to suffer more and more from this supposed disorder.

For many years, children have been born who are different from others. There is a behavioral abnormality, and that makes them ADHD children. They are more sensitive than other children and have a lot more energy and are often highly intelligent. It's unfortunate: they are not within the norm and have enormous difficulty integrating into this norm. They simply do not fit into the current system. The parents clearly find it difficult to deal with their special-needs children, and teachers are simply overwhelmed.

Personality surveys of ADHD patients from the medical centers of the great American universities found that the development of the clinical picture in these patients invariably depended on

- the age the disease was diagnosed and
- how the family or private environment, the school or workplace, responded by the time of diagnosis.

This shows again how strongly the social environment influences the patient and shapes beliefs. These conditions are particularly important for the course of the disease up to the time of taking medical measures in ADHD research today. A purely medical consideration is simply not enough. The neurobiological explanatory model must be supplemented by a psychological component.

The worst part of the whole situation is that the children are immobilized due to the excessive demands of the adults with psychotropic drugs. According to a study by the Sigmund Freud Institute in Frankfurt, Germany, 150,000 small and elementary school children are regularly among the most common in Germany prescribed the drug Ritalin. Yet this means a radical encroachment on children's lives. Their natural behavior is restricted in favor of society. The American DEA (Drug Enforcement Administration) categorized Ritalin in third place, directly after the drugs heroin and cocaine. It's just as addictive as these two drugs and has over a hundred side effects, one of the recent findings in a published long-term study on Ritalin. These are, for example, paranoid psychoses and delusions, manic symptoms, mental and physical dependency, aggressiveness, hallucinations, or being extremely withdrawn, anxiety, loss of appetite, racing heartbeat, or insomnia. If Ritalin is discontinued, it leads to depression or depressed moods, because the brain receptors are so overexcited by the drug that they can no longer be sufficiently stimulated due to a normal release of neurotransmitters, which usually occurs through real experiences. Furthermore, it is possible that the ADHD symptoms occur even more intensely than they did before taking the medication.

The "energetic child of the twenty-first century" is not sick; it is different. Ritalin restricts their urge to live and only makes them sick. Now what can parents do with their special-needs children? First off, it is important to realize that these children are incredibly special and should be treated the same way. Standard educational measures have failed. Here are some useful tips on how to deal with hyperactive children:

- Despite of all the problems and difficulties that they cause, ADHD children need a lot of love and affection. They want to see and feel it.

- The child needs the feeling of being accepted and should be told: "It's nice that you exist!"
- Praise the willingness for trying; don't praise success only.
- Increase the child's self-esteem through assigning meaningful tasks.
- Promote and praise the special characteristics and skills such as creativity, inventiveness, and spontaneity.
- Promote contacts with age-like peers. Those affected often seclude themselves out of fear of not being accepted.
- Best to focus on one task only. If possible, ask for one only, not several at the same time.
- ADHD children need a precise structure. Structuring and planning the day and setting dedicated times for individual actions.
- Establish clear behavioral rules with your child in writing. Also, formulate consequences (no punishments!) for noncompliance.
- If possible, demand rules with determination in facial expressions, gestures, and tone of voice. As example, you would explain an important rule of the DOT. Speak in a friendly and firm manner.
- Always maintain a clear position—especially when giving instructions.
- Support the communication as often as possible with nonverbal means, such as a brief touch on the shoulder. This triggers a recognition reaction in the child.
- Do not have an argument immediately after a conflict. This would lead to new arguments. End a conflict by stating facts or creating rules.
- Direct the urge for movement in the right direction. Encourage specific sports activities so that your child can release energy.
- After concentrated learning and homework, make sure the child will receive short breaks for physical activities.
- Make sure that all peers and caregivers are involved in the child's parenting. This includes teachers.

In conclusion, I would like to give you two exercise suggestions that you can do often with your special child. The first exercise is called grounding yourself. In many cases, the hyperactive child lacks a conscious connection to earth. To reestablish contact, the grounding exercise is a wonderful way to do so. You can find the exercise in the fifth part.

Here is the second exercise.

GET IN TOUCH WITH THE HEART

Hold both your hands close to the heart, about seven inches away from your child's back and chest. Close your eyes. Concentrate on your two hands only. Everything else around you will disappear. Hold the concentration until you feel that it is good. Then release your hands. You can perform the exercise often. You will feel that your child becomes calmer and more relaxed. At the same time, you will automatically increase the energy of the heart center.

RELATIONSHIPS WITH YOUR FRIENDS, COLLEAGUES, AND NEIGHBORS

> "Courageously, your counterparts make themselves available—unconsciously—as a mirror so that you can recognize yourself in them."

When it comes to relationships with all the people you encounter in your environment, it is no different than with the relationship to your partner. With this group of people too, the principles of "project platform" are working, reflection of deep issues. Conflicts within the company are often no different than conflicts at home, except the location and subjects are different. The basic structure remains the same.

Your colleague does not provide you with the necessary information and makes you look bad in front of your boss?

Your friend is constantly unpunctual, and you cannot rely on him in any way? Your neighbor shovels weeds under the fence onto your side repeatedly?

What does that have to do with you? What patterns resonate within you? It always remains the same. Would you like to solve these problems? Then look at the corresponding topics in this part to find out what fits and how you can transform it. First you should figure out and understand why your counterpart triggers negative feelings in you. Then you can start to change these aspects.

LETTING GO MADE EASIER WHEN RELEASING TIES

> "Letting go. Oh, if it only would be that easy. How easy life could be."

Letting go is one of the most difficult subjects for most people. Especially when it comes to letting go of loved ones. Some mourn their former partner for years and will not be able to have a new relationship. Others are stuck in mourning for a deceased person. Some cannot separate themselves from certain things. There are people who have cluttered their apartment and/or house, and it is so full that it's almost impossible to walk through. Years ago, I saw a documentary about these "hoarders," as they are called. When the neighbors called the police, and the police entered the apartment, they couldn't get in because the apartment was filled to the ceiling with "collectible" items. Unfortunately, it was also full of leftover food, which stank terribly. Letting go is difficult for people.

You form a bond with people with which you are intensely involved. These bonds are not always of positive nature. If these people leave your environment, this bond remains in energetic form. This can lead to unconscious behaviors that have nothing to do with you but with the former bond. Sleeping together is the most intense energetic bond you can form with another person.

There is a powerful exercise to release negative attachments to people, things, or situations, to free yourself from them. Afterward, it will be easier for you to let go.

Years ago, a woman came to me for a coaching session. She was having a lot of trouble with her mother. They rarely met in person and only spoke to each other on the phone. When they did talk on the phone, it hardly lasted more than five minutes before the conversation ended in an argument. I did the following exercise with her. After a week, she called me excitedly and said, "Siranus, you will hardly believe it. Yesterday I was on the phone with my mother. I talked to her for fifteen minutes without us having an argument." This kind of thing can happen too. When the negative ties are cut, peace is allowed to return. So anything can happen. What will happen specifically to you, I cannot predict. Just let yourself be surprised, and, as always, be free of expectations.

LETTING GO MADE EASIER WHEN RELEASING TIES

Make sure you are undisturbed for the next twenty minutes, and, as always, find a quiet and comfortable place.

Make yourself as comfortable as possible. Make sure your legs or arms are not crossed. Close your eyes, and pay attention to your breath as it comes and goes. Focus on your breath. Breathe in new energy, and exhale used energy. Feel how your body becomes calmer with each breath and your thoughts become quiet. If thoughts still arise, it's okay. Let them pass by like clouds in the sky. A thought comes and goes. You become calmer and calmer and more relaxed. All is peaceful.

Get ready for a journey. Imagine yourself traveling to a wonderful castle or palace. At arrival, you look at this magnificent structure. Somehow, you know this building. That's right, it's yours. Pass through the gate, and enter a magnificent foyer with a large staircase. Let your servant take your jacket or coat and walk up the stairs. Further back is the grand hall. Open the door and enter. At the very back of the hall, you will see a throne—your throne. Walk toward it and sit down. Look majestically around the hall, which is still empty. Enjoy sitting on your throne. Now invite all the people you have ever met in your life, all of them. There are many, but they all fit into the grand hall. Thank everyone for making the trip to be with you today. Some people you recognize immediately: your parents, siblings, aunts, uncles, and past partners. Some of them are hard to recognize, some of them are like strangers. It does not matter; they have met you somehow, somewhere in your life. The grand hall is almost full, and the last people are walking in. Thank everyone for making the trip to be with you today. Now say goodbye to those people with whom you have had only good experiences. This happens automatically. You don't have to analyze who exactly that is. Let them go. The only ones who remain are those with whom you have a negative bond. The stronger the bond is, the closer they are standing to your throne.

Feel the individual negative bonds that you have to those people. Some of these ties show up as a fine, thin thread, others like a thick rope—depending on how strong your attachment to the respective person is or was. Can you recognize all these ties? There may be many threads and ropes emanating from your body—like a spider web—a connection to every remaining person in the room. Reach next to you. There you will find a large powerful extremely sharp sword. Take it and prepare yourself to cut all these negative ties. Are you ready? Raise the sword high above you, bring it down with great force, and cut all ties!

Now feel how, while cutting, a great lightness will flood through you as a great weight has fallen off. That is exactly right: the load was allowed to go. Now place the sword aside, and feel inside yourself. What is happening right now? Enjoy this feeling and observe your remaining guests. You may see relieved faces of these people as well. It is done, these ties are removed.

Thank all of them, and let them go their way. Some of them you will see again, some you won't. Once again, enjoy this wonderful feeling of freedom and then prepare yourself to go back. But first, thank yourself that you have allowed this separation from all these people. Now leave the throne room. Walk through the foyer, let your servant return your jacket or coat, say goodbye, and go outside. While outside, enjoy the sunshine, and realize the great power that lies within the sun. Let your surroundings fade more and more, and come back to the here and now. Feel the chair, the sofa, or the bed, and become aware of yourself where you are sitting or lying. Pay attention to your breath, how it comes and goes. Take three deep breaths, and open your eyes. Rest a moment longer, and enjoy your new freedom.

QUANTUM ENERGY AND RELATIONSHIPS

The exercise "releasing ties" can be used in relation to animals, objects, or situations. When working with animals, instead of visualizing the castle, you can choose a place that you associate with the animals. To cut ties, envision a knife. For objects, have your servants carry them to the throne room. For situations, instead of the castle, visualize a large clearing in the forest. Give the individual situations their own symbols, and imagine how they appear in front of you. Again, you can use a knife to cut these ties.

Living in quantum consciousness will make your relationships much easier, assuming you use the knowledge and techniques. In this part of the book, you have received everything you need for it. Take the time you need. Start with yourself. Your matrix will change—guaranteed!

The love for oneself opens the gate to the wisdom of relationships.

I love myself!

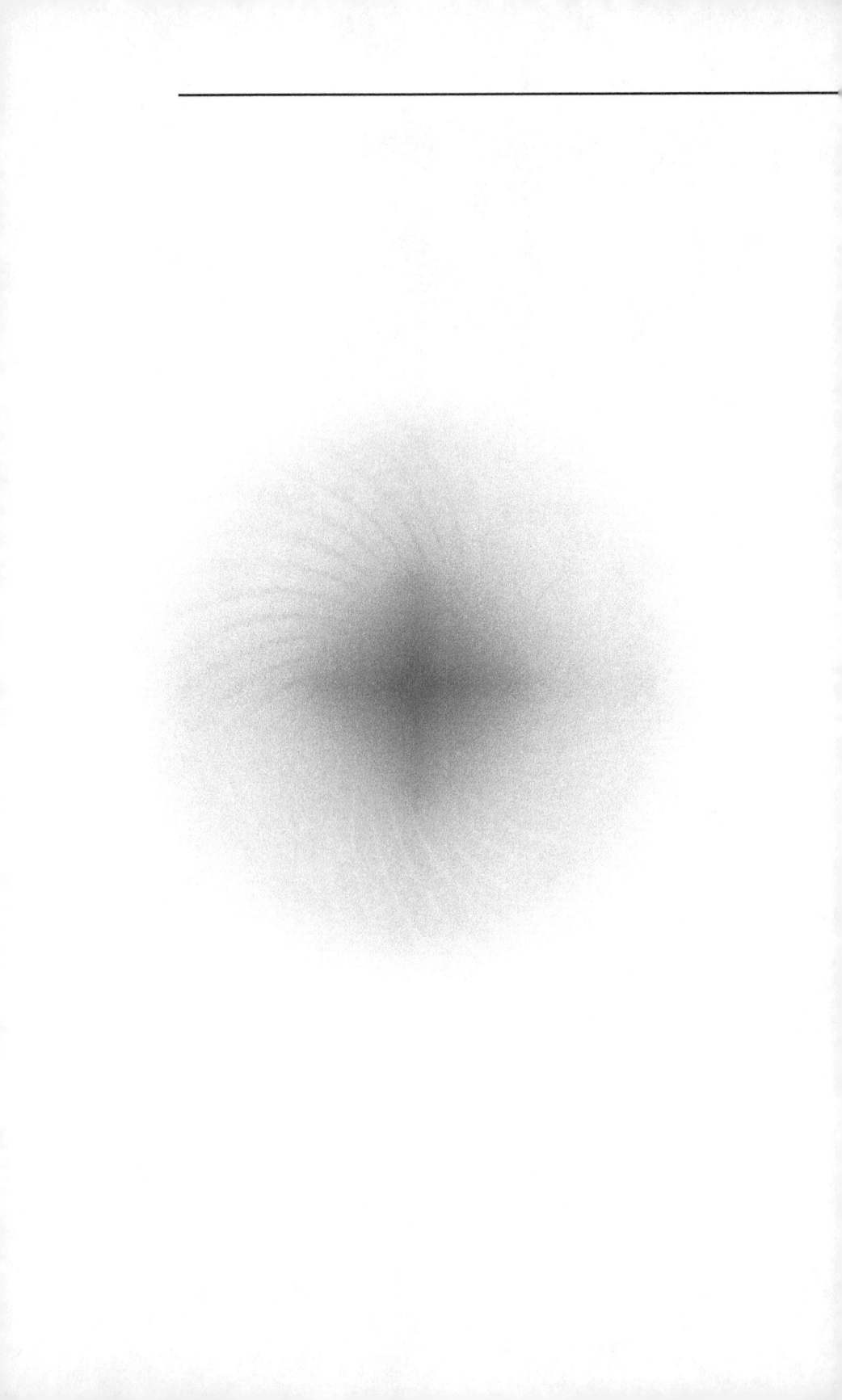

PART 4

Quantum Energy and Success/Wealth

QUANTUM ENERGY AND SUCCESS/WEALTH

> "Success follows when you follow your heart."
> —Sonja Ariel von Staden

The subject "success" has always been something that fascinates people. Almost everyone wants to be successful in some way. On Amazon alone, there are almost a hundred thousand title entries when you search the word success on German websites, almost ninety thousand of them alone in the book section. On Google are twenty-five million entries. Humans want to be successful. But what does success mean? Relevant dictionaries describe it roughly like this: Success is the achievement of a certain thing or personal progress. It comes from "to take place" and used to refer to the general consequence, the consequence or effect of an action. Everyone defines the term differently for themselves and, in my opinion, is also very important. For one person, success means taking a different route to work, then the typical way to work, while for another person, success only occurs after they have earned their first million.

I want to mention that success has nothing to do with hard work or struggle. This is a myth from the past. My experience is that success can be easy. And the easier it comes, the greater it becomes. This is one part and wisdom of quantum consciousness.

SUCCESS AND HEALING

"Success is individual."

What does success and healing have in common? For many people, healing already represents success. If healing is allowed to happen where suffering, pain, fear, or illness was present before, then this is called success. Furthermore, for many individuals, the feeling of happiness that comes with success is already healing. In my coaching's and seminars, healing happens for a lot of people when they no longer let success put them under pressure. Now it is important to address the myth of success.

THE MYTH OF SUCCESS

"No pain, no gain.
To be successful means to work hard and to struggle.
That is a myth! The new age enables us to
experience success with ease and joy."

In our society, success is very much characterized by its material aspect. Success and wealth are closely related to each other, whereby wealth is equated with financial wealth and status. Whoever has success is recognized and is something special. This is not surprising, because we come from a time of scarcity, suffering, and war. The First and Second World War have contributed to the fact that we are striving to be "successful" in the sense just described. My parents came from East Germany and moved in the early '60s to the West and started with nothing. With hard work and sweat, they managed to buy a townhome in a vacation apartment complex on the Baltic Sea. Through their accomplishment, they showed us children how to be "successful."

People strive for success to be something special and to afford something. To be successful requires hard work, a lot of diligence, and struggle. These are the thought patterns we created for ourselves from the myth of success. But how can it be that, for some, success comes with ease? People that don't struggle, who earn a lot of money with little work? Can it be that the thought patterns described above are starting to get dusty because they are outdated? There are sure many people who become successful in the conventional way. The number of those who do it differently is increasing. Many start attracting money and success instead of chasing it. Others are beginning to completely redefine success by giving it a new definition. For them, it's not just the result for success; it is also the path to it.

Myth Success...

A NEW PHILOSOPHY ON SUCCESS

"If it doesn't come easy, it wasn't supposed to happen."
—Andreas Körber

I would like to introduce you to my philosophy of success. It is simply about being successful with ease and joy. I grew up in a world in which the myth was lived. I worked my tail off to be successful, always wanted to be to be successful, always wanted to be particularly good, and then even better. For some reason, I was only mediocre, and the more I worked, the less successful I was. The same applied in school and college. I studied a lot and was only an average student. This was until someone very important to me said during my studies that I should change something: instead of always studying to be very good, I should study to be good. I reduced the standards that I have set for myself. It was not easy for me because I didn't want to be the average student and prove to others too that I could be better. Nevertheless, I followed the advice and simply practiced receiving good grades. Consequently, I took the pressure and stress off while studying and suddenly was able to concentrate better—and I got an A! I continued to follow this strategy and eventually graduated with a 3.9, wrote my thesis with a 3.5, and scored a straight 4.0 on my diploma exams. That was revolutionary for me at the time. That's how I learned that success can also be easy and doesn't have to be about struggling.

It is my philosophy that the path to success has a lot to do with fun and joy, with passion and enthusiasm. Abundance and wealth come from within and shows itself on the outside. Most people chase after money, the orders, the better-paying job, etc. I used to do that too. But it seems that money is always faster. What would happen if you turned this around and instead let money chase you? That is my philosophy of success! For me, wealth has nothing to do with money. Very few millionaires or billionaires are rich. They may have a lot of money, but internally they are often poor. Financial wealth rarely makes people happy and satisfied. It is necessary to become rich within yourself as well to move from lack to abundance consciousness.

FROM LACK CONSCIOUSNESS TO ABUNDANCE CONSCIOUSNESS

> "You have a choice: Do you want to avoid
> lack and move toward abundance?
> Do you want pain or joy? The choice is yours."

How does one succeed by moving from lack to abundance? Some folks know the law "As the inner, so the outer." Most people do not want to admit that they first must be fulfilled within to experience lasting abundance on the outside. In today's network Internet marketing boom in Germany, everyone wants to earn big money, and people are promised large sums to entice them to enter. For example, almost every day I receive an email from some online casino. However, looking at history, there are very few people who have won the big money in an online casino.

How do I become rich and fulfilled within? You will become rich within when you learn to fully accept yourself—just as you are. When you love and accept yourself wholeheartedly, you will enter the realm of inner fullness. When you take 100 percent responsibility for yourself and your life, you will be free. When you realize that happiness is right in front of you and that you only need to reach out to it, you will experience infinite inner wealth. When you shift from having to being, as the philosopher Erich Fromm[53] once described, the "needing" will disappear. Then suddenly everything will present itself. When I understood all this, my life changed radically. It

---

[53] Erich Fromm, To Have or to Be? (DTV, 2005).

seemed as if I was carried through the gate of abundance. Since then I live and experience abundance on all levels. I understood quantum consciousness without knowing what it meant. I simply recognized its laws.

Once again, review the exercises from the part "Quantum Energy and Relationships." Should the words "I love myself!" still seem foreign to you, I guarantee you that the more you work on your self-love and strengthen your self-confidence, the more abundance will come into your life.

However, there are also people who love themselves, who feel well inside, and yet live with less or not enough.[54] Why is that? It may be because these individuals carry deeply buried behavioral patterns that they are not aware of, or because they have unconsciously negative beliefs on the subject "money." Spiritual people often have a negative relationship with money. However, I would like to dedicate a separate subpart about the topic of financial wealth and come back to it later.

There is another very important aspect about the topic of lack. It could also be called epigenetically caused lack—the lack that was a result of the War.

> *When I finally understood what a tremendous power love has and its energy was released within me, was I ready to commit myself to success. Success followed my inner clarity—free of obstructive thought patterns and imprints. Thanks to this new consciousness and all the valuable experiences I had, personal success followed.*
>
> *I finally followed my gut feeling and presented to management proven facts for an important and expensive project decision, and my recommendation was accepted! A few months ago, I would never have*

---

[54] Meaning, people who live paycheck to paycheck or can't pay their rent.

thought I could do that without my inner clarity. It is fascinating what an unbelievably liberating feeling such success can trigger.

(Angelo Casciano, Rothenburg, Switzerland)

THE LACK CAUSED DURING TWO WORLD WARS

"What are you carrying on your back?" the little girl asked.
"It's the experiences that weigh so heavily on my back.
It made me hunchbacked," answered the traveler.
"Empty your backpack, dear traveler," said the girl boldly.
"When the traveler wanted to do so, the backpack was empty."

Every culture carries its history with it, and so does the German culture. It is shaped by war and suffering. Our great-grandparents experienced World War I and World War II, our parents partly World War II. They experienced lots of suffering and lack. Our parents learned from their parents that life is scarcity and a struggle, and they have passed this experience on to us. This rarely happened consciously but rather automatically and unconsciously. As a result, Germany has become a country of security thinkers. An entire industry thrives on this greatly: insurance agencies.

In my opinion, this is one of the reasons why there are only a few real successful people in this country. To be successful means taking risks, expanding your comfort zone, and trying new things. However, if you have learned to maintain security, it will be difficult for you to break new ground and to enter unfamiliar territories. Remember the life's model from the second part: only when you change your old beliefs and behavioral patterns will your life change, and lack will become abundance.

In this context, I would like to remind you once again of your self-responsibility, because in relation to the subject of success, I repeatedly encounter people who whine about their lack and think they can do nothing about it. For example, they blame the government or their life situation for it. I assume that you want to take responsibility for your life, otherwise you wouldn't be reading this book. The principle of self-responsibility is the one at the forefront of principles of the most successful people and in first place. I have studied the principles of success very intensively. There are many of them. Jack Canfield, America's number one success coach, lists sixty-four of them in one of his books.[55]

I have identified ten principles for myself:

- Self-responsibility
- Self-confidence and self-worth
- Focus
- Faith
- Passion
- Courage
- Quick decisiveness
- Action
- Constancy
- Gratitude

In my workshop "the Ultimate Success," I work intensively through these principles.

Live according to the motto: Don't complain, change.

How do you get this feeling out of your cell structure? The lack during the war, the resulting fears and "fighting for survival," mode, which does not seem to be yours but that of your ancestors.

I have developed a very profound exercise that makes it possible to release the connections from that time and to overwrite the code of the cells. I would like to introduce them to you, but this is beyond the scope of this book.[56]

---

[55] Jack Canfield, *Compass for the Soul* (Goldmann, 2005).
[56] You can order the exercise on the CD "From Lack Consciousness to Abundance Consciousness" at Amazon or at my online shop at www.quantumenergycoaching.com.

YOUR FOCUS DETERMINES YOUR SUCCESS IN LIFE

"Energy follows the attention. So be mindful of your thoughts."

The subject focus is my favorite topic because it is very powerful and easy to use. I told you about the law of attraction or resonance. It states that you attract what you focus your attention on. If this is indeed the case, then you probably know why your life has turned out the way you have experienced it. Most people know what they don't want in their lives. Only a few know what they really want. But what do you think happens when they focus on exactly what they don't want? They get exactly that. The law of attraction always works, like the law of gravity or the law of cause and effect.

So if you always put your focus on what is not going so well in your life instead of what's going well, what do you think will multiply like a virus? The not-so-good things, of course. If you get tired of seeing your extra pounds in the mirror, what do you think will happen? You will gain even more.

If you're always upset that you're receiving so many bills and your debts are getting higher and higher, what do you think you will receive in your future? More bills, of course, and a growing mountain of debt. Many know this principle as the "self-fulfilling prophecy."

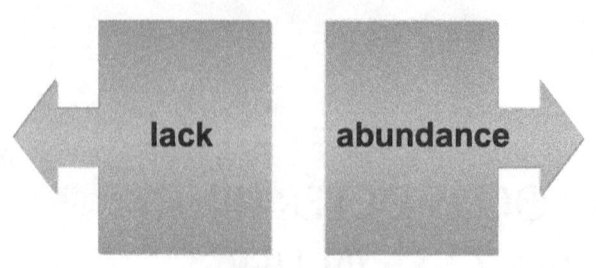

QUANTUM ENERGY AND SUCCESS/WEALTH

What do you focus on?

Starting today, you have the option of focusing your attention on what you don't want or on what you do want. The decision is up to you.

It is your focus that decides about happiness or unhappiness, success, or failure.

You decide. Go back to yesterday in your mind, and find out what you were focusing on. What did you fabricate through it?

FENG SHUI FOR THE BRAIN II

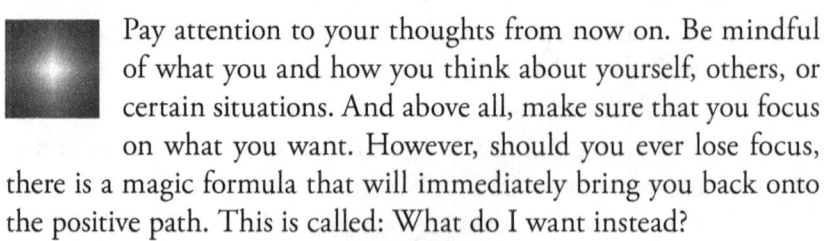

Pay attention to your thoughts from now on. Be mindful of what you and how you think about yourself, others, or certain situations. And above all, make sure that you focus on what you want. However, should you ever lose focus, there is a magic formula that will immediately bring you back onto the positive path. This is called: What do I want instead?

If you ask yourself this question, your attention and your energy will focus on the future, not on the past. Because that's exactly what happens when you focus on what you no longer want. You are looking back.

So what do you want instead?

Here comes an exercise that extends the "feng shui for the brain" exercise and can make a big difference in your life.

SEVEN DAYS THAT WILL CHANGE YOUR LIFE

Starting today, make a resolution to spend one week paying close attention and to focus exclusively on the positive things in life. Start doing this when you wake up, and end it when you go to sleep. If you lose focus in between, use the magic formula: "What do I want instead?"

This is a very challenging yet powerful task which requires a lot of discipline and mindfulness. However, after the week has passed, you will notice that a lot has changed in your life. I also recommend finding someone with whom you can do this exercise with. That way, you can keep reminding each other to pay attention whenever you lose focus. This makes the task much easier for you.

BE THE CREATOR

"If there are any laws for success, the following is number one: Take 100 percent responsibility for your life."

I would like to start this part with a story. Lisa is a woman who likes to go shopping. Not long ago, she was strolling through the city and suddenly stopped in front of a store window. She saw a painting, a true work of art. She was so fascinated by this painting that she forgot time. After ten minutes admiring the painting, she gathered all her courage and went into the gallery. Again, she was so smitten by the painting, and her heart was warm and fuzzy. The salesperson noticed Lisa's enthusiasm, approached her, and told her a little about the painting. Lisa couldn't get over her enthusiasm and already imagined leaving the store with the painting, hanging it up at a special place in her house, presenting it to all her friends. She had already fallen in love with this painting. Finally, she asked about the price. The salesperson replied, "Two thousand euros."

Lisa's enthusiasm faded abruptly, and she thought, *Two thousand euros—never can afford that.* She thanked the salesperson and left the gallery disappointed. The dream of owning it quickly vanished.

She could not forget about the painting. She walked past the gallery for the next few weeks, stopped, dreamed about owning it, until the price came back into her mind.

Time passed. Four weeks later, Roxanne passed by the gallery, saw the painting, and stopped in her tracks. By just looking at it, she felt in love with it, just as Lisa did. She went into the store knowing that the painting was about to become hers. The salesperson approached her. She asked for the price and got also a sticker shock. For her too, a painting in that price range was unaffordable. She knew that she wanted this painting. It was already so deeply anchored in her heart that it was crystal clear for her that the painting would soon come into her possession.[57] So Roxanne asked whether she could reserve the art and whether there was a way to pay for it in installments. The salesperson replied that this was not a typical sales procedure, but, because of her enthusiasm for the painting, he was going to ask the owner of the gallery. He promised Roxanne to inform her about the owner's decision as soon as possible.

Two days later, Roxanne received the important phone call. The salesperson told her that she could pay for the painting in six installments of €333 each. This was exactly the amount Roxanne could afford to pay each month. She was overly excited and would have certainly hugged the salesperson if he had been standing in front of her. Beaming with joy and excitement, she went to the gallery, bought the painting, and planned a party in its honor.

Back to Lisa. One Saturday evening, when she went to one of her friend's parties, she turned pale when she saw "her" painting hanging in her friend's living room. Tears welled up in her eyes, and she left the house immediately. The other guests uncomprehendingly watched her leaving.

How often have you buried a dream because you were afraid to act on it? What made you hold back? I wasn't any different in the past. Today I know that when I really want something with all my heart, it will come true. Presuming I fully commit myself to it. This, of course, does not mean that you should now irresponsibly spend your money on everything. I am only pointing out that people limit themselves when they think that something is not possible.

Act and take full responsibility for what you want for yourself and your life! You are the architect of your own reality. You yourself create your day every day new. So you have the choice to dream or to bring it into your life. Become an expert in quantum consciousness. Use your creative power.

---

[57] In my book *Bring Light into the Darkness of Your Belief System* (Schirner Publisher, 2012), I describe this clarity as the "unshakable belief system."

QUANTUM ENERGY AND SUCCESS/WEALTH

One of my training participants used her power of creation in a slightly different way. But read for yourself:

> *We are owners of a small mechanical engineering company. My partner made an important appointment with an interested customer, and I suggested to coach him a little bit. It became a mix of different "quantum energy" exercises. Although I did not have to remove any fears for him and did not want to give him anything with a different shape, look or feel, as we had learned from you for anxiety release, I still adapted this model:*
>
> *I crafted a "success outcome" and visualized it accordingly. I applied the exercise to synchronize the matrix field to get the necessary information. As with the exercise for anxiety release, I was visually holding an object in my hands.*
>
> *It was a beautiful four-sided pyramid in malachite green, about ten inches high, with some gold dust on the top—like fresh snow on the mountains surrounded with some clouds. After visualizing all of it, I located a place on his body that felt good to place the image. I formulated my intention, stepped aside, and left the rest to the universe. When my partner returned from his appointment the next day, I was astonished. The chance for this order had been approximately 20 percent. That the interested party would even sign the purchase contract on the same day had a 3 percent chance. But he did.*
>
> *(Sandra Reichmann, Stans, Switzerland)*

THE PHYSIO-MAGIC

> "Only when you are aware of the magic of the
> universe can you create anything."

About two months ago, my trainer colleague and friend Thorsten Weiss asked me to write a foreword for his new book *Spiritual Money Awareness* (Schirner Publisher, 2012). I read his manuscript to get an impression of the book. It appealed to me very much, so I decided to write the foreword. One part particularly caught my attention: "Physio-Magic." I never had heard of this term before, but the name alone made me curious. Thorsten Weiss defines physio-magic as a kind of miracle-working illusion that originates from your creative imagination to support the physicality of your dreams and fantasies.

What exactly does it mean? Quite simple: In the exercise "activation of self-healing power," you have already visualized and blended your imagination and reality. This leads from imagination into being. The physio-magic goes a step further. But I better let my dear friend speak for himself. When he wanted to become a healer, he opened a practice and had no clients. Nobody knew about him, and he had a realization. He wondered what a day of an extremely successful healer would be like. Of course, he had thought about it in advance, but he did not only want to think like a successful healer but also wanted to act like one. Because of his cancer treatments in the past, he knew the hospitals well, so he went on a visit. What comes next almost left me speechless. But read for yourself:

> One morning I set out to go to the clinic. I
> knew the oncology department of the University

Hospital in Tübingen inside and out. I knew exactly where my workplace was for that week. I parked my car not in the visitors parking spaces but in the special designated area for nursing staff and physicians. *If I'm going to do it, I'm going to do it right*, I thought to myself. After that, I walked in with the attitude of a passionate healer with confidence of someone who has the courage to follow his life's passion. I walked into my workplace. I went to the floor where people were receiving chemotherapy as outpatients, waiting to be picked up by the radiology staff to undergo radiation therapy. This seemed like an appropriate place for me. I sat down between all the waiting and desperate people and started my work. For hours I connected with my inner healing source and gave the people what I felt they needed at that moment. I gave them all my attention they needed, the appreciation. I admired them and opened my heart. I touched them in their hearts with my love and let all the gratitude for my life flow to them. I asked for forgiveness. I connected with my power and gave them the same ability. I meditated, I observed, I supported, and I just did what a healer does all day when people come to his practice. For lunch I went to the cafeteria and sat with the doctors and nurses. I walked around in the clinic as if I was at home there. Crazy? Maybe. But it worked. And that gave me strength to go on. I did this for almost two weeks, and I had fun and enjoyed it. During my breaks in "treatments," I wrote down a waiting list with any names that came to mind and, underneath, things like: "Be sure to call back when new appointments are available." And what happened? The phone started ringing for my own practice. Sporadically at first and then more and more. My appointments were taken, and, after a few months, my practice was fully booked. By doing this, a mechanism was set in motion that made me attract more into my life what I was already doing. This is real magic! It is not a fantasy. It is real. Physio-magic is nothing else than treating your environment as you would treat it as if you were the person in your desired reality.

Isn't that amazing? This is using the law of attraction to perfection. And for this reason, I don't want to deprive you of physio-magic. Use the exercise "activation of self-healing powers" into "the wishing well."

THE WISHING WELL

1. Think about which wish or dream you want to come true in your life.
2. Close your eyes, and concentrate on your breath as it comes and goes. Feel how you slowly relax.
3. Imagine the desired state with all your senses. It does not matter how far away you are from this state at this moment.
4. Dive into the source consciousness until you feel that it is good.
5. Feel your dream being already fulfilled. What happens when the dream is reality? What do you do? How do you live? How do you feel? How do others talk about you? How do you think about yourself? Who is with you?
6. Feel the situation so strongly that imagination and reality become blended. Experience everything up closely. Be the desired situation!
7. When the feeling is the strongest, press the index finger and thumb of one hand together for about five seconds, and anchor the feeling in your hand movement.
8. Give thanks for the wish that has already been fulfilled.
9. Come back to the surface of your now consciousness.
10. Write down in details what you have experienced.
11. Test your anchor by pressing your index finger and thumb together again. Does that indescribable feeling arise again?
12. Repeat the exercise at least twice a day for the next thirty days, but you do not have to set the anchor again.
13. Consciously let the new reality flow into your everyday life. Consciously act as if the wish were already a reality. Just as

Thorsten Weiss did. Move forward courageously! If possible, surround yourself with everything that belongs to your dream.[58]

14. If doubts arise, which can happen, release your anchor.

It could be that you feel embarrassed when doing your exercise and others will look at you funny and ask what you are doing. Don't let this discourage you. The more you are convinced of your dream, the faster it will become reality. And the more you enjoy the view from this somewhat unusual "summit," the more prepared you will be for other unusual things in your life.

As you may know, only those who walk in fresh snow can leave behind footprints. The typical roads that everyone travels on soon become icy lanes. To express it according to my philosophy: be different, not the norm!

---

[58] A few years ago, I arranged for my wife's birthday a test drive in her dream car. Because the price tag was way out of our budget at the time, she was still able to—without purchasing it—experience what it's like to drive this car. There are always options. Think beyond common possibilities.

THE WHY IN YOUR LIFE

"Without a WHY in your life, life is meaningless."

If you have aligned your focus on the positive in your life and this has become part of your daily routine, the next task is to focus this alignment even further on what you truly want in your life. Most people have never dealt with this question. As stated above, many know what they do not want. However, only a few have ever asked themselves the following question: What do I really want in my life?

This question is essential because if you don't have a WHY in your life or nothing that drives or propels you, you are just going through the motions. Real successful people constantly ask themselves the question of their why. They have the "big idea," as the Americans call it. They have a big vision. They have goals to which they align themselves to.

There is a wonderful story about this. A professor of motivational psychology is on a quest to find out what these people's inner drive is. During a vacation, he meets a construction crew. He asks the first construction worker: "What are you doing?"

He replies somewhat gruffly and bad-temperedly: "Can't you see that? I'm cutting stones!" A bit confused, the professor walks on. A few minutes later, he comes across a construction worker that seems to be in a better mood. The professor asks him what he is doing.

The worker answers: "I'm working on a stone that needs to fit perfectly into the space over there. I need to be very precise and accurate. Every 1/16 of an inch needs to be correct. Because I can work with such precision, I'm employed here."

"I see, that's interesting," says the professor and goes on his way.

At the end of the construction site, he stops in amazement. He sees a construction worker who is happily singing a song and halfway dancing along as he goes about his work. "Do you also hammer stones?" the professor asked.

"But no," he replies, as shot from a pistol. "I'm working on a cathedral. Can't you see that?"[59]

What is your "cathedral"? What is your life's work? You don't have a cathedral yet? I can reassure you, only a few people do. Even if you say that your cathedral is still not more than a small village church, that's perfectly okay too, because you can expand your church. You can add high towers, make the inside beautiful, add a special staircase, and make it a reality. Your idea will become a vision that will attract more things magically.

Scientists have discovered a while back that 80 percent of all motivational energy comes from a personal vision. You need to have an inner drive to get up every morning, otherwise you will remain a masonry construction worker for the rest of your life. The bad thing is that it's not you who determines your path but that you are led by your outside, by your environment. That is completely fine if you're happy with it. But I assume you are not reading this book because you are completely at peace with your life. A living vision ensures that you get up in the morning with joy and start your day. It contributes to the fact that your work is fun and nourishes you with a sense of achievement. Genuine self-motivation arises from an attractive vision of your own future. By the way, your vision may already seem quite unrealistic at first glance.

How many visions have become a reality in the past even though, at first glance, they seemed absolutely utopic. Bill Gates was laughed at when he stated that one day every household would have a PC and his software. Today no one laughs at the idea anymore, and he is one of the richest people in the world. Another example is Nelson Mandela. His vision gave him the strength to endure several

---

[59] S. Sven von Staden, *Handling Sovereign Changes within Thirty Minutes* (Gabal, 2010).

years in prison. Soon after he regained his freedom, he became president. There are so many other examples: Henry Ford, Walt Disney, the Wright brothers, Oprah Winfrey, or, from recent history, the developers of Google, YouTube, or Facebook.[60]

The power of vision, the why in your life, is the engine that drives you, the force that makes you—like Nelson Mandela—step through deep valleys to shine brightly and arrive radiantly at the summit.

The Vision

What is your vision, your "big idea"? Why do you get up every morning? What do you really want in your life?

---

[60] Mark Zuckerberg certainly never imagined that nearly a billion people would use Facebook one day. He had been relentless in his commitment to his vision.

WHAT DO I REALLY WANT?

Take a pen and notepad, or download the template for this exercise at www.quantumenergycoaching.com in the download area.[61] Ask yourself the following question: "What would I do if I would not be afraid? What would I do if all my dreams and wishes came true?" Take plenty of time to think about this question, especially if you have never dealt with the subject before. Often, the deepest longings and desires are hidden and buried deep within us because we don't believe they could ever come true. Many people may have told us too: "You can't do it," "It won't work anyway. "Who are you to want to do something like that" etc. If you are familiar with these phrases, ignore them for now.

By the way: The how is completely irrelevant at this moment. You can worry about the HOW later. Now, it is only about the WHY. Spell everything out. Start dreaming and give your dreams free reins. Awake the child within you. As a child, you knew nothing about limitations. Should the critic in you speak up, give him time out. He deserves it because he speaks up often enough. Let everything come up and let your imagination run wild.

Place your pen and notepad next to you and close your eyes. Visualize everything you just have written down as if it would be already a reality for some time. Imagine your dream in all kinds of colors and details, feel it, see it, taste it, everything that belongs to it. Listen carefully. Let the sounds, noises, and voices also free range. Feel how it feels that all has been coming true. Let this feeling flow through your whole body, through every single cell. Flood your

---

[61] Go to the website www.quantumenergycoaching.com, register, log in, click on "Downloads." You will find all resources for the book.

cells with this wonderful feeling until they are completely full. Then anchor this incredible moment by pressing your left thumb and index finger together. Feel how this entire feeling is projected into your hand movement. Release your hand position after five seconds and indulge in your dream for a moment longer. Now, speak the following sentence in your mind: "Thank you that this is already true." Then open your eyes, and enjoy your smile, I bet it's already there.

Repeat this exercise once a day for at least thirty days. There are people who do this for months and incorporate the exercise into their daily routine—as a normal part of their day, such as brushing their teeth. Should your vision for any reason disappear, which I do not expect, then use your anchor. Press your left thumb and index finger together. That wonderful feeling will come back, and you will be able to revel in your vision again.

THE VISION BOARD

Extend the above exercise. Buy a large picture frame that is worthy of your vision.[62]

Get a few old magazines, newspapers, or use online images and cut out pictures that match exactly your vision. You may have a few photos you could use too. Place them on your picture frame. When you have completed your vision board,[63] hang it up at a place that you feel it's worthy of it. This could also be the restroom. After all, that's a place where you would see your vision board several times a day.

Look at it often and revel in your vision and think about the exercise "what do I really want?" Make time for it, even if it is only a minute. Is your vision worth a minute? I hope so!

The power of a vision/dream board

---

[62] You decide on the size.
[63] Are you a perfectionist? You don't need to buy new magazines in the hope to find the right pictures. Take something that matches. It doesn't have to be exactly the "right" picture. That is not what matters here.

As you can see, I have many pictures on my vision board. Some people recommend using only a few pictures on a vision or dream board so that the energy does not get deluded. My vision/dream board is from 2010. Despite the many aspects listed on it, half of it has already come true. I don't know about you. I think two years is an immensely short time for a vision to be fulfilled.

So what are you waiting for? The best thing you can do today is to create your vision board and benefit from its power. The prerequisite is, of course, that you firmly believe in the fulfillment of your vision.

> *I must share something with you! Do you remember my vision board? Kissing dolphins and starting my spiritual school? This summer we're going to Florida. I got a voucher to go swimming with dolphins. Vision 1 is therefore as good as fulfilled. But now it is getting even better. I have applied for a course as "spiritual educator" in the field of "spiritual pedagogy." Yesterday I had my staff review meeting. During the meeting, we started to talk about continuing education. I told the members about my vision and about this training. Can you imagine: Both school board members, absolutely non-esoterically, were enthusiastic. They asked me to get in touch with them when my training is completed, because they want to consider incorporating what I have learned into the public school system. Getting the community involved and on board. Isn't that unbelievable? So vision 2 is on its way.*[64]
>
> *(Nadia Ravljen, Mettmenstetten, Switzerland)*

---

[64] Nadia had created her vision board only three and a half months earlier.

YOUR BIG THREES

"And when someone asks you at the end of your days "What have you done with your life?" what will you answer?"

Now that you have your vision, it's time to take it a step further. Let's say your lifetime is up, and you had only one more day to live. You would reflect on your life.

You probably would ask yourself questions like these:

- How has my life been?
- Am I satisfied with the way my life has turned out?
- Have I been happy?
- Did I do everything I could do?
- Did I achieve my goals and visions?
- Did I fulfill my desires and live my dreams?
- Etc.

How about asking yourself these questions not at the end of your days but today? On the last day of your life, you can no longer change anything! You can only plan on doing things differently in the next lifetime—if you believe in reincarnation. How often do I meet older people who mention in our conversations: "If I only had…"

Would you like to make the same statement someday? You have a chance to change your life here and now so that you can answer the above questions with a smile on your face, so you can say to the creator, "I am ready!"

At this point, I don't want to go into all the questions mentioned above, but I would like to ask you another one that could become your constant companion:

What are the three major goals that you would like to see fulfilled in your life?

What are the "big threes" in your life?

People used to say: "Start a family, build a house, plant a tree, and drive a BMW," or something like that. I think the BMW thing was different back then, and it would have been the fourth goal. However, I have added the BMW on purpose because it is completely okay to have a material goal as well.

My big threes are as follows:

- I live a fulfilled life in prosperity and live my day the way I like it.
- I live and work in the most beautiful places on earth.
- I support millions of people with my potential to live a fuller, healthier, and happier life.

Today, toward the end of 2012, three years after I set these big threes, the first two have already been fulfilled. If all keeps going like this, the fulfillment of the last goal should not take much longer. This is the incredible power of the big threes in combination with the implementation of quantum energy and the aspects of action.

Now it's your turn.

MY BIG THREES

Take all the time you need for this task. Have a pen and notepad ready. You can download the template for this exercise at www.QuantumEnergyCoaching.com.[65]

Soul-search and ask yourself which ten goals, things, or projects you want to achieve, accomplish, or carry out in your lifetime. What is important to you? Write everything down, even if it is more than ten. After spelling everything out, take another close look at your notes. Ask yourself honestly whether they are really all of them or whether some are nice to have or do but not necessary. Cross out the ones that are not in the top ten. Now ask yourself if these items are really yours or if some of them are aspects that others (e.g., parents) expect of you. It should only be yours. Often we live goals and carry out projects that are not ours at all. Too often we do these only to be recognized or liked. Cross out all goals that are not yours!

Now evaluate your list. What is the most important goal or project? Create an order. Now feel within yourself again until the order feels coherent. Now take your big threes. Are these the ones? Are these the three goals to which you will be saying in ten years' time: "Yes, those are my big threes!" Now create a table or download the template for this at www.QuantumEnergyCoaching.com. In the top row, write down your three goals. In the column on the far left, enter the areas of your life—health, relationships/partnership, success/profession, personal/spiritual development.

Assign one to five points for each goal in these areas of life. Zero points means that you cannot achieve your goal/project in this area. Five points means that you can achieve and integrate the goal/

---

[65] Download information. See footnote 61 on page 201.

project in this area. Remember the motto "Love it, change it, or leave it."[66] After the evaluation, you can decide how you want to deal with them. Have you given four or five points? Wonderful! Have you given fewer or even zero points? Then think about what you can change to increase your score. You may consider that it does not fit at all to either let the goal go or to continue with it as before despite the low score because you still love it. In any case, the table content is a good indicator for the achievement of your goals or projects.

---

[66] "Love it, change it, or let it go (or leave it)."

Table Content

Life Area	Goal 1	Goal 2	Goal 3
Health			
Partnership			
Career/Success			
Self-Development			
Spirituality			

DEFINE YOUR GOALS

"The most expensive luxury yacht is worthless if the captain doesn't know the sea."

Have the clear goal in mind.

Successful people are successful because, in addition to a vision, they also have written goals that they clearly pursue. You can read about this in almost every success book. Do you have next to your big threes other written goals? Short-, mid-, and long-term goals? In all areas of your life? If not, then write down the following questions:[67]

- What is my monthly goal in terms of (1) health, (2) relationships, (3) finances/career/success, (4) personal development/spirituality?

---
[67] Or download the template at www.quantumenergycoaching.com.

- What is my yearly goal in terms of (1) health, (2) relationships, (3) finances/profession/success, (4) personal development/spirituality?
- What is my five-year goal in terms of (1) health, (2) relationships, (3) finances/profession/success, (4) personal development/spirituality?

Use a separate sheet for each goal, and write down what you will do to achieve that goal. What do you need to accomplish this goal? Who do you need to reach out to? Create an action plan. Whereas with the vision, the how is not important at first, but, with your goals, you should be very action oriented.

And, of course, to make your goals more easily achievable, you may want to incorporate the source consciousness.

GOAL ACHIEVEMENT SIMPLIFIED

As you prefer, sit on a chair or lie down on the couch or bed. Close your eyes. Breathe in deeply a few times, and notice how you relax with each breath. When you feel deeply relaxed, visualize your goal as if you have already achieved it. See your achieved goal right in front of your eyes. Now step into the picture so that you are in it. Do you feel like you have achieved your goal? Pay close attention to how you feel. Now go into the source consciousness, and speak the following words in your mind: *Goal easily achieved.* Stay in source consciousness for a while and feel within yourself. What has changed? When ready, slowly come back to your now consciousness, and open your eyes.

Going forward, be attentive to the signs that appear on your way to your goal. Often the strangest circumstances arise that lead you closer to your goal. Sharpen your perception for these impulses and signs. In the part "Quantum Energy and Spirituality," you will get to know an exercise on how you can significantly increase your awareness for these impulses and signs.

In my workshop "Live Your True Greatness—Now!" I worked with my participants and taught them an exercise that enables them to turn a goal into a magnetic goal. I would like to introduce you to this exercise as well.

Do you know the situation where you have a goal that you want to pursue, but somehow you manage to do something else instead of staying on task? Many may have that challenge. The following exercise makes a goal extremely attractive and appealing.

THE MAGICAL ATTRACTION OF THE GOAL

Find a place, preferably outdoors, that measures at least twelve feet in length and where you can walk freely with your eyes closed without getting hurt. Position yourself so that the free space is behind you. Then close your eyes. Visualize your goal as if you had already reached it. What do you see when you have reached your goal? Who is with you? Where are you? How are you dressed? Imagine every detail. What do you hear? Sounds, voices? Can you hear yourself talking?

Now go inside your picture. Experience it "live," having reached your goal. How does it feel? Where in your body do you feel it? Absorb this feeling and enjoy it.

When you are completely emerged in the feeling, imagine attaching a strong rubber band to each of your shoulders. Now step out of the situation and see yourself at the finish line, standing with the two rubber bands at your shoulders. Attach the ends of the rubber bands to your shoulders so that you are connected via the rubber bands to your goal/target. When the rubber bands are well fastened, go backward very carefully and slowly, and notice how, with each step, the rubber bands tighten more and more. Go back as far as you can until the rubber bands will prevent you from taking another step back. The tension may cause you to lean forward. In this position, recognize how your goal literally pulls you forward and becomes more attractive. Now place your hands on your shoulders, and anchor the pulling feeling into your hand movement. Release your hands from your shoulders when you are ready, and enjoy the moment and the feeling of being pulled toward your goal.

Now walk toward your goal again, and release the rubber band from your shoulders. Open your eyes, and walk around a few steps. Think about something else for a moment. Anything. Then think about your goal again. Is it more appealing to you now?

If, for some reason, your goals vision should ever become less, then place your hands on your shoulders as you did in the exercise and release your anchor. The vision should appear again.

To conclude the subject of goals, I would like to add something that I read in the book *Success Is Not an Accident* (Ariston, 2010) by Noah St. John, which I like very much.

Three reasons why we fail to achieve goals:

1. We strive for something we really don't want. That is, we pursue goals that are not ours at all (but the parents, partner, etc.) Ask yourself if the goals are really your personal ones.
2. Our goals are unattainable, outdated, or unrealistic.
3. We do not allow ourselves to stop setting goals. We do not take time to enjoy the goal we have achieved, but immediately set the next one, acting according to the motto: "Higher, faster, further."

ACTIVATE POTENTIALS THAT ARE NECESSARY FOR ACHIEVING YOUR VISION AND GOALS

> "Dive deep into the sea of yourself, O seeker, to recover the greatest treasure there is: you!"

I often discover that most people are not aware of the potential they carry within themselves.

In our everyday life, we use only 4 to 5 percent of our potential.[68] But, with the help of source consciousness, you can activate the untapped potential. Because you are connected to everything via the unified field, you can also tap into the potential of other people. If you allow yourself to see the universe as a big department store, then you can pick from all the shelves and get what you need in that moment.

In the movie *The Secret*, this possibility is compared to Aladdin's magic lamp.[69] We ask the genie in the lamp to make our potentials available to us, and the genie says: "Your wish is my command!" It is supposed to be that simple? Yes, just as simple as that.

Life is generally easy. We have just never learned to take it so lightly. That's why we tend to make life infinitely difficult for ourselves.

First I would like to show you how you can uncover your unused potential.

---

[68] See page 10.
[69] *The Secret* (Goldmann, 2007, page 41)

UNCOVERING YOUR OWN UNUSED POTENTIAL

Which potentials and abilities do you need to realize your vision or to reach your goals? Create a list. Write down all the skills you think you need to achieve your vision. Then do the kinesiological test to see which potential you need right now.[70] To do this, ask yourself the question "Do I need X (for X, set the potential or the skills) to achieve my goal/vision?"

If your fingers are hard to separate, you are on track of the right potential. If it is rather easy, then perhaps the desire is there, but there is no real need.

Then stand in front of your bed or in front of an armchair so that you can fall softly backward in case you need to. Should it be necessary during the exercise and/or you have the feeling of being pulled backward or that your knees become soft, then you can fall safely. This may happen in the middle of the exercise, but this is perfectly fine. In my seminars, it has happened often that participants have fallen over before I have even started. At that moment, it was enough just thinking about the result. The impulse collapsed the energy wave that was building up, causing the participant's system to reorganize and moving the tangled information back into its original position, into the primordial matrix. The same thing can or will happen to you. No matter whether you fall or not. The falling over is only a possible result of restoring the primordial matrix.[71]

---

[70] The exercise for this can be found on page 36.
[71] See the first part.

Now think of the potential you want to uncover (e.g., courage, serenity, inner peace, strength, etc.). Place a hand on your body part that comes to mind intuitively or where you feel your hand belongs right now. With your other hand, feel in front of you or sideways in your energy field and feel where the potential is. It is already in your energy field. It may be that you feel a slight tingling sensation or that suddenly something is different than before. Perhaps your inner voice is telling you where the right place is.

Your knees may become soft, and/or you have the feeling of being pulled backward. Give in to this impulse. At this moment, you are simply aware of your two hands. You may feel the source consciousness. This arises automatically. Think briefly *Potential released*, and enjoy the moment.

Notice what is happening. If you have fallen over, stay down for a moment. If you have the feeling that not enough has been released yet (trust your inner voice), then repeat the exercise a few more times. I recommend you repeat the exercise for a few days.

Recognizing the potential within the energy field.

Welcome to quantum consciousness. The effect of this exercise is based on the principle of entanglement. You intertwine the energy

QUANTUM ENERGY AND SUCCESS/WEALTH

of one hand with the other. This causes the energy wave to collapse, and your body may react by falling over. My seminar participants love to "fall over." A nice side effect is that the compulsion to control yourself is to loosen up, because when you fall, there is no longer any possibility of control. Unless you force yourself to keep standing up.

> *I've been working with my husband, Thomas, in writing down all our visions. My long-time vision has been that we would no longer keep farm animals (we still had five mother cows), but instead build a "retirement home" for animals (cows, goats, sheep, donkeys, etc.) that runs on a donation basis. For a whole year, I have been looking for a solution, but somehow, I just couldn't get anywhere. My husband, on the other hand, had the vision that we could keep more horses on our farm. So, with these things in mind and with the help of "quantum energy," we integrated all the aspects we needed and wrote everything down. What happened within the next two weeks was unbelievable. Suddenly we got a request if we could take in old and orphaned goats and sheep, which would be financed by donations (my vision). At the same time, we got so many requests from horse owners who wanted to place their horse with us (Thomas's vision). Because we can only realize one of both visions at this time, we had decided for the horses. Now we are already building an extension to accommodate a larger herd, which will be ready to move in by June! By that time, we will be financially able to separate from the mother cows so that we no longer have any farm animals. I am so glad because I'll never have to say goodbye to a calf again because it's going to the slaughterhouse!*

And two weeks later:

> *So much has changed again at our farm. We are expanding our horse boarding facility and will hire someone that will allow me and especially Thomas to have more time off. That is so great! A few weeks ago, this would have seemed somehow utopian to us.*
>
> *(Heidi and Thomas Risi, Buochs, Switzerland)*

A CLEAR DIRECTION

"Draw your sword, O warrior, and point its tip toward your path."

I often experience individuals who are very creative and have many ideas but lack a structure, a clear direction. I just returned home from a workshop that also made it very clear to me about the necessity to not lose focus in all my projects. Once again, it is about the focus or, rather, about directing the focus on where the most energy is. Here's an example from my life:

When I decided in 2009 to use the economic crisis as an opportunity to further expand my private seminars, I clearly focused on it. The result was my first workshop "Live Your True Greatness—Now!" which was completely booked within a few weeks with forty-two participants. I was very enthusiastic and continued to put all my energy into it, and the next workshops were completely booked as well. This showed me that a clear focus leads to success. This explains the fact that energy follows the attention.

The vision of my wife and I to realize our dream at the end of 2011 was similar: to move our area of activities somewhere to paradise—in our case, to Bali. From 2012 on, we would spend most of the year living on the "island of the gods," as it is called and known.[72] Here is the story:

In March of 2010, we spent our vacation in Bali. In knowing that we wanted to emigrate there, I made contacts through the

---

[72] Now that the book's expansion is complete, my wife and I are living in Ibiza. Bali remains the focus, but we have both learned to listen to the universal impulses and signs. We will stay in Europe for the time being.

Xing[73] network with Germans living in Bali. From ten I approached via email, five answered. We also searched where we could live and where suitable premises for our seminars were. Equipped with a clear vision and the first contacts, we set off for Bali. The law of resonance took care of the rest. As soon as we arrived on the island, we made the best contacts we could ask for. We met an entrepreneur who organized a brunch for Germans in Bali every Sunday, and through him we met other important people. We found beautiful premises for our seminars. On the last day, we met a real estate agent who showed us our dream house with pool and directly on the beach. The property was offered at a price that was a tenth of what we would have paid in Germany. We could not get out of our amazement. When the realtor mentioned that he would keep this house available for us until the end of 2011, my jaw dropped. The miracle was perfect, because we had prepared a crystal clear vision for ourselves.

How many people have a similar vision of emigrating and experiencing a harsh reality because they either do not follow through due to negative statements of others, or because they don't follow their impulses and prepare in a structured way?

So if you have a vision, take advantage of the opportunities that the world offers you. Use the wisdom of quantum consciousness. And listen to your inner voice. Blind actions have never helped any vision to reach its goal.

Back to my seminar subject. My alignment led my seminars to being completely booked. But what else happened? This focus led to all my other projects having zero energy. All my other business contracts disappeared. I wasn't aware of that at the time. I initially attributed this result to the economic crisis, but I later realized that it had to do with my focus.

If you focus your full attention on one thing or one project, the energy of the others become much weaker. Less happens there, or in my case, nothing happened at all. What do you think happens to people who juggle several projects at once? You have distributed all your energy among various projects. As a result, all the projects

---

[73] Xing is one of Europe's largest Internet business networks: www.xing.de.

are running mediocre. This is understandable and one of the reasons why success coaches advise you to focus on one thing and to become an expert in it. Not focusing on anything, but rather focusing and being great at one thing.

How do you manage to focus your energy? Here is an exercise that will make it much easier for you.

THE CLEAR FOCUS

Think about which project or goal you want to focus on in the future.

Stand in a place where you can spread out your arms. Close your eyes. Just recognize how you are standing there. Then focus on your energy that is around your body. You may simply notice it. You may envision a certain color, like the aura of the human being. No matter what it is, perceive it. It may take a moment. At some point, you will feel the energy around your body. Now visualize your project or goal an arm's length in front of your eyes. The easiest way to do this is to assign a symbol to it and imagine the symbol. Take your stretched out arms as far back as possible at shoulder height. With the palms facing outward, you can reach further back. Then bring your arms forward at shoulder level, and "scoop" your energy in front of you until both arms are stretched out in front of you. Now all energy is bundled between your arms and directed toward your project, like a laser beam. Let the solar plexus (center of your body) or heart energy flow into this "laser beam" in the form of light so that it is amplified by both energies. Speak in your mind "energy flows powerfully." Now your focus is crystal clear, directed like a "laser beam" on your project or goal.

Notice what is happening within you. It may be that you feel a lot, or you may feel nothing at all. No matter what, it is good. Then let go of your vision, open your eyes, and be excited about what just happened. Now leave the rest to the law of resonance.

QUANTUM ENERGY AND SUCCESS/WEALTH

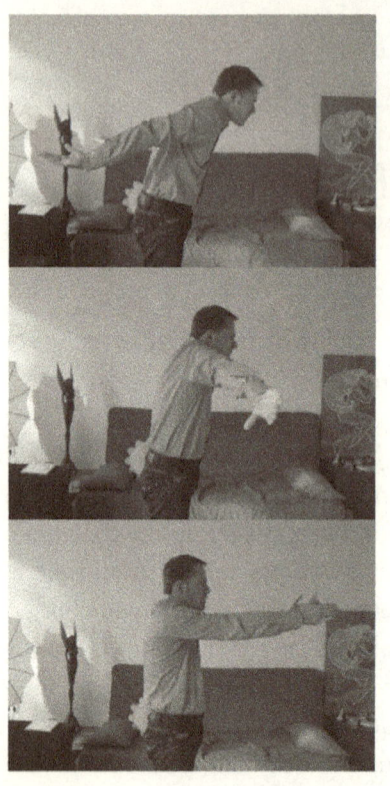

Focusing the energy and directing it toward the goal.

Whenever you feel you are losing your alignment toward your goal, you can repeat this exercise and transfer light and information to your goal. It is important that you pay attention to the impulses and signs that arise in your life in relation to your projects or goals. If you are clearly aligned with it, there will always arise these so-called coincidences that come to you and bring you one step further. Open your perception to them, and listen to your intuition. Too often we overhear these impulses and signs. So become attentive. In the part "Quantum Energy and Spirituality," you will find an exercise that will improve your perception of these impulses.

STRENGTHENING STRENGTHS— THE PATH TO YOUR CALLING

> "When the calling becomes your profession,
> there will only be paid vacation."

Germany is a country of security thinkers. This is due to our past. Unfortunately, this circumstance has led, I suspect, to the fact that we have fundamentally misunderstood something in our cycle of learning. From our parents, and especially in school, we learned to improve at something we are not good at. There are tutoring services for children who are not so good in a specific subject. In school tests, all mistakes are marked in red. Our social system puts the focus on what is not working so well and works on compensating these weaknesses. I bet you remember well how time-consuming and difficult it was for you to compensate. Oddly enough, this is done differently with highly gifted children. In their case, their talents are promoted. Why only the highly talented and gifted?

In this book, you have read quite a bit on the subject focus. What happens when you focus your attention to your weaknesses in order to eradicate them? That's right, they become stronger. That is the reason why it is so exhausting to improve or compensate for this weakness. What would happen if you were to treat yourself like the gifted ones and allow yourself to focus only on your strengths and talents? Of course, these would become better and better.

The principle of "strengthening strengths" is certainly not unknown. And yet only a very few people use it. Apply it in your life as well. The most successful people are so successful because they concentrate only on their talents and develop them even further. Michael Schumacher was good at many sports, but his special talent was in Formula One. This led him in the past to emerge as the winner in many races.

What are your special talents? What are you particularly good at or better than others? What comes easily to you? Continue to develop this talent, and, if you are brave enough and have the courage, turn it into your profession. If you allow and trust yourself to do this, then your calling will very quickly become your profession. If you follow your talents and calling, then every day will feel like a paid vacation. Then, at some point, there will no longer be any difference between your job and your time off. You will start each day with joy and will blossom in your work like a rose showing its full splendor to the world.

I have been living my calling for quite some time now, have taken the chance to do what brings me absolute joy. Otherwise, I would not have been able to spend days and weeks to work on this book that you are holding in your hands today. One thing I can assure you of: it is impossible to earn money any easier than with your calling, because you are on a permanent vacation, so to speak.

You lack the courage to do it? In this book, you have learned many exercises that will enable you to integrate and transform everything that prevents you from doing so. Act! No matter what you decide, the decision is always the right one. For that moment. Even if you do not decide, that is still a decision.

TRANSFORM YOUR BLOCKAGES IN REGARD TO SUCCESS

"Think what is unthinkable, and do what seems impossible. Your success will be unstoppable."

What have you learned about success? What have you learned about "you" having to earn money? How is success defined for you? Does the myth of success apply to you? How did your parents model success to you? What did the media contribute to it? Does your life for success resemble a struggle? How have you been shaped regarding success? You only need to look at your past to see what your imprints look like. If you want to change your beliefs and patterns that are limiting you, then you can do that with the exercise "changing beliefs." Change your beliefs, and you will change your life.

Everything is possible.

QUANTUM ENERGY AND SUCCESS/WEALTH

The following exercise gives you another opportunity to transform or remove blockages and obstacles on the path to success. But before you work on changing it, ask yourself what the blockages are for and what they want to point out to you. Be curious and learn to understand yourself better. There is a reason for everything, including your blockages about the subject of success. Do the exercise "making contact" first.

TRANSFORMING BLOCKADES THROUGH YOUR OWN CREATIVE POWER

One option to transform the blockages and obstacles is to take your own creative power to help you. Make yourself comfortable, and close your eyes. Become aware of yourself. As in many other exercises, feel yourself as you are standing, sitting, or laying down. Then pay attention to your breath as it comes and goes. Let your breath guide you into a relaxed state of mind. Feel how your daily routine is fading away more and more, your shoulders are relaxed, and your entire body becomes heavier and heavier.

When you feel completely relaxed and your mind is calm, get in contact with your obstacles, blockages, and see them clearly in front of you. Feel the power that your blockage radiates, the power it has over you. Now remember that God has created you in his image and likeness. Imagine yourself walking fully into your creative power. Take the time you need to do this, and build your power up more and more. You are a creator; you are great and powerful. Feel how more and more power is flowing into your body. All the power that has been asleep in your energy field is suddenly awaking and flowing into your body. Recognize all your power. Your cells are flooded with your power, your energy.

(If, for some reason, your power does not increase, get in contact with your solar plexus. Let its yellow light energy flow through you and wrap your entire body. Can you feel the power now?)

When your cells are refueled, let the blockages reappear in your mind. It may be already difficult to do so. If they are still present, use your creative power, and let the images of the blockage fade away. Just like clouds in the sky that become thinner and thinner until they are completely disappearing. When the picture of the blockage has disappeared, move on to the next blockage, should there be any others. Use your power to create a radiant picture of a world of success, like a bright blue sky.

When all the blockages have been transformed, focus on your breath again as it comes and goes. Come back to the here and now, and open your eyes.

Can you still feel your creative power? Now do the self-test. Imagine your blockages once again. Are they still there? Do they still have power over you? If yes, then repeat the exercise. Test again in a few days. There are two possibilities. First you can no longer find an image or resonance. Secondly, the resonance is still there. In that case, it may be that your subconscious mind was powerful enough to retrieve the blockage. If so, do the exercise for thirty days, every morning after waking up and every evening before going to bed. This will ensure that not only the original matrix will be restored but also that permanent neurological networks are allowed to develop.

At this point, I would like to introduce you to another exercise for the transformation of your limiting beliefs. You can test which exercise you find easier to do. Either the visualization exercise, the "transforming your creative power," or the following:

Consider in advance what the so-called "instead" is regarding your limitation: What should your belief be called so that it is beneficial to you? Let me give you an example. If your belief is "only the others are successful," then your positive counterpart could be "success is mine." Or instead of "you have to work hard for success," you could say "success comes easily and consistently to me." Leave all negativity out; just state your positive intention.

REPLACE YOUR BELIEFS IN THE MATRIX

Think about which limiting belief, which set of beliefs, you want to change. Now ask yourself what you want instead, what your new positive belief is, and write it down on your notepad. Now close your eyes. Feel your energy field that is around you. You may feel a vibration or even perceive something slightly in your mind. As soon as you can recognize it, sense in your energy field where the limiting belief is located. Somewhere in there is a vibration stored. You may need a moment to locate it because it is unfamiliar to you. Give yourself enough time, and follow your intuition. It knows where the vibration can be found.

Now where in your energy field do you perceive the new beneficial belief? When you have located it, do the following: With one hand, consciously remove the limiting belief from your energy field, and throw it far away from you. Immediately after, replace your new belief, and place it in the position where your limiting belief was located. Now feel and perceive what has changed.

That's it. Too simple, you think? It is just as simple with quantum consciousness. I always introduce this exercise in my workshop "Live Your True Greatness—Now! and experience many astonishing and beaming faces afterward.

Now test how well the exercise worked for you. Imagine yourself in a situation in the future in which your former belief would have hindered you.

How does it feel—still limiting or more beneficial? Based on this feeling, you can tell if something has changed. Should the feeling still be negative, then repeat the exercise once again. The result should be that a visualized future situation should feel neutral or ideally positive.

> *I have a client who came to me because she felt like she was going to lose everything and considered to end this life. Her life was one big fight. Struggle with her husband, her kids, fighting with her parents and her sister. Everyone was picking on her that everything she did was wrong. She felt guilty for the depression of one of her daughters. Her job gave her a stomachache and made her nauseous every day. Still she had to keep going because her parents told her that she was the problem and that she shouldn't make such a fuss about everything.*
>
> *In the initial conversation, it quickly became clear why she was attracting all these things into her life. She blamed herself and felt guilty for all the miseries of her family members. The father of her children did not pay the child support because "she wasn't worth it" and "she didn't deserve it." At least that was what she had internalized. First we changed the most dramatic beliefs and integrated self-confidence. Then together we formulated her power questions that she can ask herself every day.*[74]
>
> *Within two weeks, she had unconsciously managed to be terminated from her "stomach-aching job" and found a new one. She found herself a new family law attorney, who has been helping*

---

[74] Power questions are originally affirmations that are transformed into powerful questions. Read more about this in the book by my wife Sonja *Ask Yourself Happy—How POWER Questions Can Change Your Life* (Schirner, 2012).

her get justice ever since. Today she no longer feels helpless and takes matters into her own hands. The relationship with her parents and her sister is now able to heal. She is enjoying life again.

(Petra Kinast, Langenfeld, Germany)

TRANSFORM PROFOUND BEHAVIORAL PATTERNS IN RELATION TO YOUR SUCCESS

"Success is human."

As already mentioned in the parts "Quantum Energy and Health" and "Quantum Energy and Relationships," there are also very profound patterns in the subject of success which have their fixed place in the cell structure. Because the approach is like "Quantum Energy and Health." Just exchange the subject and then do the exercise accordingly. You will notice afterward that a lot has changed.

EXPERIENCE WEALTH ON ALL LEVELS

"The problem of the poor is not the lack of money. Even if you were a millionaire, you still would be poor if you feel lack internally."

I would like to conclude this part with reflections on another myth—wealth. It is quite exciting to see how we chase after the beloved money. This is a phenomenon of all industrial societies, the so-called First World. We are designed for materialism, and so money has one of the highest values. For Indigenous peoples, such as the Aboriginal people, money has no importance at all. How much power do we give to this form of payment, and how much time in our lives do we spend chasing money, only to spend it? I don't want to go deeper into this subject because it would clearly go beyond the scope of this book. I would like to make you aware of how strongly you are influenced by money.

I have already made you aware that before you achieve external wealth, you first need to achieve internal wealth.

In this part, it is about how you can significantly increase your money flow. I would like to start with what is holding you back from making a lot of money. I often meet people who have tried an infinite number of things but only have enough money to survive. I also have participants in my coaching sessions who manage to build "wealth."[75] But just as the money flows in, it flows right back out. Not because those individuals have bought themselves something nice; it's because either an extra bill arrived, taxes were due, or the car needed repair.

---

[75] For some people, having $1,000 in the bank account represents wealth.

These people can do whatever they want. The money that comes in goes right back out. There is nothing they can do to prevent this from happening. Do you know these situations from your own life or from people you know?

If I ask these individuals whether or not they do want to have money, they deny it and, on the contrary, finally admit that they want to live financially in abundance. What I then tell them, however, most of them do not want to hear or believe. I make them aware that their statements are not true. In that moment, all I see are question marks on my clients' faces, which I can understand. I like to believe that they want to have wealth on the conscious level, but, on the unconscious level, they reject money. Once again, that's how tricky our minds are. We mean yes and yet say no. Now what could be the reason for subconsciously rejecting money? You can uncover this quickly with a few questions:

Ask yourself the following:

1. What have you learned about money?
2. What have you learned about rich people?
3. How was the lack anchored in your parents?
4. How did your parents or those who raised you talk and think about money or rich people?

In my workshop "the Master Plan," I work out a strategy with my participants on how they can bring into their lives what they want. We look at, among other things, the participants' belief about money and rich people. I would like to mention a few different statements as well:

- Money is the root of all evil.
- Money does not grow on trees.
- There is something dirty and bad about money—like the people who have a lot of it.
- Money stinks.

- The rich get richer and richer, the poor get poorer and poorer.
- Rich people can't be trusted.
- Rich people have mostly acquired their money illegally.
- Rich people have oppressed others to get their money.
- Money corrupts character.
- Money creates arguments within the family/marriage.
- Men need to make money.
- You can't make a lot of money and be spiritual at the same time.
- Save money for a time of need.
- You must save for a rainy day.
- You must work harder to earn more.
- You must earn money the hard way.
- The pursuit of wealth leads to stress and health problems.
- The pursuit of wealth leaves little time for anything else in life.
- I am not good/intelligent enough to be rich.
- You can't have it all.
- Life is a struggle.
- You need to earn your money.
- Everything has a price.
- Nothing comes from nothing.
- Money doesn't make you happy.
- We can't afford it.
- Money is not that important.

Save now, and you will have in time of need.

Do you know some of these statements? Probably most of them. Do you believe, with such beliefs, you are able to earn big money? Most likely not! Let's look at some of these examples:

- If you have learned that money is the root of all evil, how good is it for your subconscious to have money?
- If money doesn't make you happy, what's the point of having money for your subconscious?
- If you must earn your money, how hard do you think you have to work for it to get a little bit of it?
- If rich people can't be trusted because they acquired their money illegally and had to oppress others to do so, what would happen if you were rich yourself? Of course, you would do the same and have to behave the same way. Do you think your subconscious mind would like that?
- If you save in time to have when in need, what are you saving for? For need, of course. So you are working with your earned money to have more need.
- If money is not so important in your life, what do you think will it do? Shine with absence, of course. If you would tell your partner tonight that he or she is not so important to you, they will probably start packing their bags. And so does the money.

Can you now understand why you can try as hard as you want? With such beliefs, you cannot get anywhere. Rich people have different beliefs. They perceive being rich as completely normal. Donald Trump, one of the richest people in the world, once lost almost all his money because of a mistake. Within just two years, he had even more than he had before. We are not talking about a few million here. You can add a few zeros to that number.

One of my teachers once said, "There are two groups of rich people: first, those who have inherited or won their money, and secondly, those who have earned it. These two groups are very different from each other. The one who has earned their money, you could place them somewhere naked and without any possessions. Within a short time, they would become just as rich as before. The ones from the other group would quickly freeze or starve to death."

This is understandable because they have no idea how to earn their money. It is statistically proven that most lottery millionaires have less money than before after about five years of their win and are often in debt afterward. The other group of rich people remembers very well what strategies they used to make money. Read the biographies of those individuals and be inspired by them and then find your own strategy.

Especially in today's world, the chances of becoming rich are higher than ever before if you change your beliefs, learn from the best, and have a strong desire in getting rich. For all you penny-pinchers, I'd like to share an advice from the wealth trainers of the world: Money is not for hoarding. Money becomes more when it is in flow. That's why it's called money flow.

You already know how to change your beliefs. If there are any fears about money, use the exercise to free yourself from fears and transform them.

But how can you change your money flow? I am glad to introduce you to a few exercises, but you should only perform them when you have changed your beliefs and fears. Otherwise your money flow will continue to be thin.

CLEAR THE FLOW OF MONEY FROM OBSTACLES

I suggest you sit on the edge of your bed or sofa so you can comfortably fall backward after the exercise. If you prefer to do this exercise while standing up, I can give you a few exercise variations. Close your eyes, and visualize your cash flow. How does it appear? How do you recognize it? Look very closely: Is anything blocking your money flow? Whatever is blocking your money flow, remove it and relocate this obstacle. Then reach into your energy field and tear down this obstacle so that the money flow is free again. Look closely. Is there anything else that is slowing down your money flow? Like rocks in a river, rocks that slow down the water flow. If you see rocks, remove them! If they are too heavy, remember your power and take them out.

If the river is full of mud, remove it. If your river is narrow and like a small stream, reach into the stream and widen it so that the river can flow freely. Be creative. Whatever image you have of your river, change it by actively intervening in what is happening—that is, in your energy field. Should your primal matrix reestablish itself or the flow is suddenly so strong that it knocks you over, allow it to happen. You will fall softly.

This exercise may sound like child's play, but it has a decisive effect. In your energy field, the stagnated flow of money will be evident accordingly. If you actively make a change as described above, you will change the energy in your field. The original matrix is allowed to restore itself because you became active.

INCREASE THE MONEY FLOW

Stand upright and close your eyes. Focus again on your money flow, but notice only the energy of the flow, not the flow itself. How does it present itself to you? If it's rather dark or black, then change the color to gold. If the flow is rather light and small, then increase the flow, like turning on a faucet on high. If the flow is narrow, then expand it, make it wider. All with the power of your imagination.

After that, go into source consciousness. Dive deep until you are completely immerged in your consciousness. Stay there a few minutes. State a firm financial intention such as "Money is always abundant," "My house is already paid in full," "I am financially free," "Money keeps flowing to me in many unexpected ways," etc. Always state your intention as if it has already happened. Then remain in source consciousness for a moment, and come back to your now consciousness.

Money flow significantly increased.

Be free of expectations, and leave it up to the universe how your intentions will be fulfilled. Don't try to force any changes. The more you let go of the issue, the more opportunities will arise for your intentions to come to fruition. This does not mean that you could not be active. Pay attention to the universal impulses that come to you, and act on them. (In my case, for example, it was the idea to write this book about "quantum energy." When I wrote it in 2010, I knew it would be successful. Within five weeks after print, it was a bestseller at Schirner Publishing House (and so are my following books). Often the strangest situations arise in which we cannot recognize first that they will lead us to the desired money.

Do you know the difference between financial independence and financial freedom? At some point, I thought it was the same thing. But it's not. The difference is striking. When you are financially independent, you can pay your rent, go out to eat, go on vacation, etc. So you can afford it. However, if you are financially free, then you can do whatever you want. After this was explained to me, I wanted to be financially free. Before that, it was always important to me to be financially independent, without knowing that I already was. I thought that, in order to have that freedom, I would have to be a millionaire. One day I woke up and realized I am financially free!

I do what I feel like doing every day, go out to dinner with my sweetheart, go on vacation several times a year, and have fulfilled most of my dreams. Yes, today I even live in Ibiza, Spain. And all of this without being a billionaire. Everything depends only on your attitude and actions. I earn my money with what I enjoy the most, surrounded by people who love what I do, live in a sunshine state, and work when it suits me. Life is great. Do you think you can do the same? Absolutely. Set a goal to be financially free, and be certain that there will always be more money than you need.

An advice at the end of this part: when you meet people who are already living the abundance you desire, bless them. That way, instead of being envious or sad, you will find joy in abundance. First for others, then finally for yourself. Because joy magically attracts abundance!

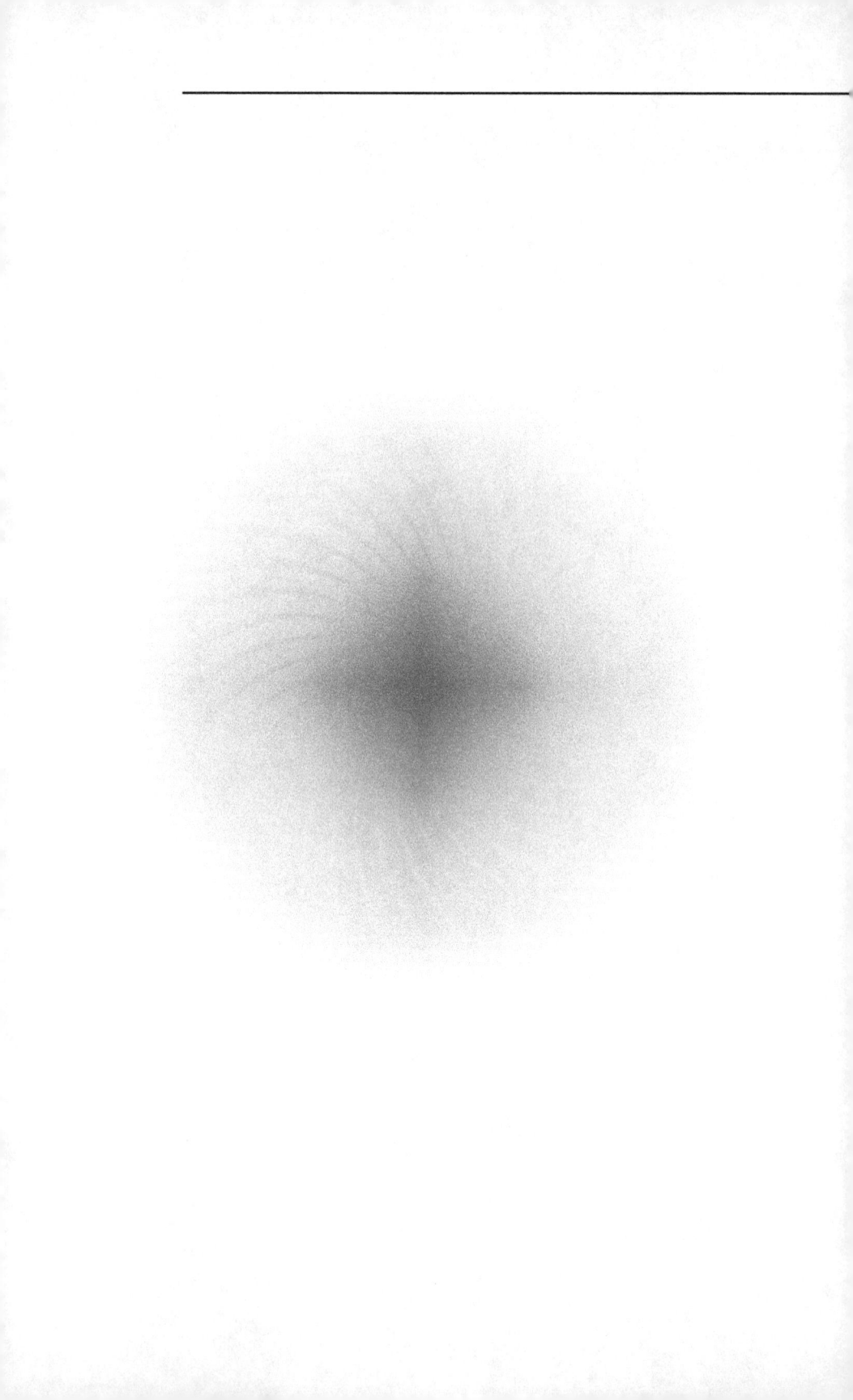

PART 5

Quantum Energy and Spirituality

QUANTUM ENERGY AND SPIRITUALITY

> "What if there was an answer for which we wouldn't have a question yet?"

"Quantum energy and spirituality" is a method that can be used for one's own spiritual growth. Whereby spirituality, in many ways, is viewed as something big and, by others, dismissed as esoteric or the "other stuff." Therefore, I would like to clarify first what spirituality means and how I use and define the term for myself. Relevant lexicons describe it as follows: Spirituality (from Latin *spiritus* "spirit, breath" or *spiro* "I breathe") means, in a broader sense, "spirituality" or, in a deeper sense, one's own spirituality with a religious meaning. For me, spirituality is more corresponding to the English term "spirit," for the spirit or a mental being. This can also be of religious nature but not assigned to a certain religion. The term stands for conscious preoccupation with questions about the meaning and value of our essence, the world, and its people. Spirituality should be tangible for everyone and be easily understood. This part deals with questions that people ask themselves more often today.

SPIRITUALITY AND HEALING

> "Stop searching for the beauty in the world when
> you have it right here in your heart."

When spirituality means dealing with the essence of our being, then this term has a lot to do with healing.

Many people come to me because they are in search of themselves and in search of success, abundance, health, etc. In that moment when you go from searching to finding, healing will take place. "I would like to" becomes "I have" or "I am." When you understand that concept, you will have an expanded consciousness. You will step into the field of quantum consciousness. Your ability to act and change anything grows enormously. This also means healing. The moment you are completely one with yourself and have accepted yourself as you are, peace and serenity will take place. Healing can happen. I could continue this list forever. Spirituality and healing are close together they almost seem to be inextricably linked.

As a life coach, I also work with tarot cards. In the context of the analysis and a look into the depths of the soul, I was already able to have extensive experience in the years of my work. Since I have deeply internalized the quantum consciousness, I can feel how my perceptions are more intensified. Instead of using my tarot cards during my phone coaching, I receive important messages prior and during the day. The energy flows powerfully.

(Myriam DioRa Haug, Bad Homburg, Germany)

THE QUESTION AND MEANING OF YOUR LIFE

"Find your gift, and the search is over."

"What is the purpose?"

Many people ask me in my seminars about the meaning of life, one's life purpose or their destiny. In all the years during my spiritual work, in the search for the big why, I have come to the following conclusion: the purpose of mankind is to enjoy life.

Neale Donald Walsch, author of the book *Conversations with God*,[76] speaks directly to my soul. All the searching for something special comes to an end if we manage to find joy in every single

---

[76] Neale Donald Walsch, *Conversations with God Volume 1* (Arkana, 2006). A recommendation for all of those who do not know what to do with the term God. In this book, God is demystified and understandable for everyone.

day—joy in the small and big things evenly. Giving joy to others as well. Many of us find it difficult to feel joy and happiness. The reasons are complex. Part of it I already described in this book.

In addition to life's joy, there is, in my opinion, another purpose. Everyone has a special gift, a special talent, something they can do better than others. If they are dedicated to promoting this gift, using it for the good of the world, they have found their destiny. Whether it's Wolfgang Amadeus Mozart, Walt Disney, Oprah, or Mahatma Gandhi—they all followed their special gift. So if you want to find your purpose, then ask yourself the following questions:

- What am I really good at?
- What is easy and effortless for me to do?
- What can I do better than others?
- What gets me excited when I do it?
- What makes me so focused in the process that I forget everything around me?
- What makes time fly by?
- What things are extremely easy for me to do?
- What do others say about me that I do well or with ease?
- What is my special gift, my special talent?

There are probably several things that come to mind. Above all, remember your childhood, because our talents were often not encouraged, possibly even forbidden. Write them down, gather them all up, find out if there are commonalities. Where are the matches? Focus on strengthening and developing your gift. You will notice that this will go rather easy, as if you receive support from somewhere. This alone shows you that you are on the right path.

For your gift too, I would like to share an exercise with you from quantum consciousness which will provide awareness to support and awaken your hidden potentials that support your gift.

AWAKENING UNUSED POTENTIAL TO STRENGTHEN ONE'S OWN GIFT

Stand with your back in front of your bed or an armchair because the energy you activate may make you fall backwards. Just think of the words "Strengths of my X."[77] (Use your gift or talent for the X.) Place one hand on your body part that comes to mind intuitively. With the other hand, feel (with a stretched-out arm) in front of you or to the side of your energy field and feel where the energy of your potential is located. When you feel your potential, just focus on your two hands. Nothing else. Just think *Potential uncovered*.[78] If you feel you must fall backwards, let it happen.

Enjoy the pleasant feeling of quantum consciousness. If you feel that the exposed potential is not strong enough, repeat the exercise a few more times. You can also repeat the exercise every other day.

With daily repetition of this exercise and meditation, one thing became clear in my heart: I realized again what I am living for.

> *Meeting others and dialog is something that is especially important to me, that moves me deeply inside and above all gives me a lot of joy. On March 16, 2012, I created and opened the "Room for*

---

[77] For all those who do not figure out what your talent or gift is or do not know how to integrate it into everyday life and earn money with it, I have an intensive workshop developed. "Follow Your Calling" is held once a year in Ibiza, Spain. You can find more information about it on my homepage: www.siranus.com.

[78] With the thought of these words, you put an impulse into the unified field. It's therefore enough to think about it once.

Encounters and Exchanges." Therefore, I planted the seed that was such an important path in my life. It was just the beginning; however, it brought me so much joy. Since then, my life has changed. It has become much more colorful and livelier. The best thing is that the people, events, and information come to me. I don't have to go looking for them anymore.

My deepest heartfelt wish for my fellow human beings who are surrounded by hopelessness is to greet them with an open heart and to guide and accompany them to their essence—to be a spark in the dark, so to speak. The HOW, I leave it to the divined plan. I have the confidence that my intuitions will guide me and that a method to do so also will.

(Beyhan Yücel Wechsler, Sursee, Switzerland)

RECOGNIZE YOUR INDIVIDUAL SPIRITUALITY

"There is only one way: yours!"

On my spiritual journey, I have met with different teachers and encountered different traditions. There were teachers that had thousands of followers, while others had only a few students. There were also people that asked me: "Are you a student of...? For a long time, I followed a certain spiritual tradition because I thought that was exactly the right way.

I never was that active, dedicated student. Somehow I felt it was not the right way for me. I've learned a lot, what I am very thankful for, and I still apply things today that I've learned during that time. Therefore, I am certainly a student in my own way. Yet it means being an active student faithfully following a path. It didn't feel right for me. In my opinion, human beings are not there to go someone else's way but instead their own path. Of course, you can use methods and techniques that you have found and learned elsewhere. But you should keep asking yourself whether this will fit your way, and, if so, how you can make it your own. In my case, instead of developing "quantum energy," I could have it done easier by using "quantum healing" by Dr. Frank Kinslow or "matrix energetics" by Dr. Richard Bartlett or "reconnective healing" by Dr. Eric Pearl. But a voice inside of me said, "Go your own path. Develop your own method. So I did, and I felt the strength that lies within when you are doing your own. All my life I followed the footsteps of others because I did not have enough self-confidence to go and do it my own way. But the power that developed by doing it myself was much bigger than doing it someone else's way. For that reason, all my participants in my training as a quantum energy coach can develop their own method. With this book, you too can find out which of the many exercises work best for you and which are the most successful ones. You've probably already realized that the exercises, slightly modified, work for many topics, subjects. That's exactly why you learn many different techniques—so that you can figure out what works best for you.

Knowing your own spirituality means going to find your own way. This works in the most challenging and easiest and wisest ways at the same time: finding you!

What does this general statement mean?

- Start to work on yourself more often.
- Find out why you are who you are, and reflect on yourself and your behavior.
- Notice how you react in certain situations and why you react that way.
- Realize what your fears are trying to tell you.
- Feel within and ask yourself what your needs, desires, and dreams are.
- Bring this into your life.
- Find your destiny, your gift, your greatest talent.
- Follow your passion and your vision.
- Start to accept yourself more for who you are.
- Be honest with yourself and your feelings.
- Start loving yourself.
- Go into silence, meditate, go into nature, etc.
- Learn to let go of the past and focus on the here and now. Right now you can make changes and decisions that affect your future.
- Become an active architect of your reality. Design your life the way you want it.
- Take full responsibility for yourself and your life.
- Learn to listen to your intuitions—your inner voice.

Realizing all these goals is certainly a life's work. And, of course, it is not a question of addressing all aspects at the same time. Yet "to find oneself" means the everlasting contact with yourself.

In our everyday life, we are often so busy and concerned with other things that the contact with ourselves is subordinated, and we are just "functioning." Turn your outside focus inward, and you will "find yourself" faster than you think. You can use the exercises in this book to tackle these issues. For others, you may need some assistance. Myself, I am always looking to get support so that I am consciously aware of my own blind spots.[79]

Everyone pursues these aspects differently. There are people that meditate every day in front of an altar for a long time. Others go into nature. Wherever you go to get into silence is completely irrelevant. Some do not meditate at all and still "find themselves." "Every dude is different," as they say in Cologne, Germany. There are thousands of ways to find and live your own individual spirituality. **But in the end, there is only one way: yours!**

Go within yourself - meditate

---

[79] Blind spots are aspects of our being that take place unconsciously; for example, early on learned and hidden patterns that we have forgotten about that are still shaping our lives.

BECOME FREE OF RATINGS, JUDGMENTS, AND GUILT

> "Go out and find the ones with the real truth. Your life will be over before you will find them."

We have already worked with the subject of guilt in this book.[80] We are often seeking someone to blame for what happened to us. Therefore, however, we only distance ourselves from our own responsibility for our life and become the punchball of others. Please remember: our outside only reflects what we carry within ourselves. If something happens or affects us and it is not good, then it is only happening because there is a vibration within us. Just today I had a phone conversation with a client that asked me why others would bully him. I could only give him one answer, and that was that he had to look at himself and what the situation may have to do with him.

That doesn't mean that it was his own fault. But if I investigate what this is all good for and why this is happening to me, then I have the chance to change something. Don't get angry, but change. Maybe you've been in a job for a long time, feel uncomfortable, and the universe, through bullying, allows you to finally exit and to look for something new. True. Apparently, you have wanted out of this job for some time but have been too scared to look for something new. Here you go, here is an opportunity. We don't always have to understand everything. But if we take the time to deal with such situations and look deeper, then the chance is great that we literally see the light at the end of the tunnel.

---

[80] Starting on page 131.

Guilt or accusation leads to relinquishment of personal responsibility and not to change. Act in your own behalf. Use the wisdom of being the architect of your own reality. Change the script of your life.

The situation is similar with the subjects of "ratings" and "judgments." We evaluate things and people all day long. It's no wonder because we live on earth in duality; there is always good and bad, light and dark, etc. But who says that something is good or bad? Who is right about this? Everyone, because everyone believes his or her own world and what he or she says is correct.[81] But what would happen if all ratings and judgments were dropped? Then suddenly everything would be as it is. A beautiful woman would be the same as a woman that is considered ugly. The "cold Northern" German would be the same as the warmhearted and open Rhinelander. The chairman of the board and the housekeeping employee would be the same. There would be no difference anymore. And if there was no difference, we would not need to play roles anymore in order to be "perfect." How simple life could be. And imagine what it would be like if you still found yourself judging someone, and you would say to yourself, "Oops, busted. Next time I'll do it better." I claim that I rate or judge humans seldom. And still I catch myself doing it—unconsciously. We all are only people, so it is just a matter of recognizing more and more how we react to ourselves and our environment. And the more I pay attention to judging myself and others less, the easier life will become. For me and others.

The next time you catch yourself judging others, ask yourself the following question:

What does that have to do with me?

You will probably find out very quickly that your counterpart is only a "project platform," a mirror or even a hidden pattern within yourself.[82] And that's great, because, without a counterpart, you may

---

[81] Think about the Life's Model.
[82] The subject on projects, mirrors, and dark patterns, you will find on page 133.

not even realize what's going on within you. Learn to let yourself and others be as they are. All is well, and it's not your job to change others. And before you judge yourself, rather admit and say: "Yes, that's how I am right now. That's me too." And if it is necessary, change it next time. Everyone is, by nature, a person full of light and love, free from tangled information. It's just that our actions may be inadequate for others. Your job is to grow. You can only grow by making mistakes. From these mistakes, you learn—every day, over and over.

In 2009, I had the opportunity to see the Dalai Lama live. I will never forget what he did when the presenter was speaking to another guest; he acted like a little child and played with his feet in front of tens of thousands of people.

Did he care? Absolutely not. He just enjoyed it. And everyone was happy for him. His holiness is certainly a prime example of being free of judgment—to oneself and, of course, to others. And nevertheless, there may be situations for him where judgment will happen. We are all just human.

THE EASE OF "I AM!"

"And if you want to achieve something, you've already lost it."

We live in a society in which we want to be perfect. We are constantly striving for something new or special. True. Apparently this is because we want recognition. Therefore, it is often about "higher, faster, further." And the further we go, the faster we do things, the more we lose sight of the special things that constantly surround us—the flowers on the roadside, the careless play and joy of children, the traveling clouds in the sky, etc. When we have set ourselves out on the spiritual path, we are looking for something special—ourselves. I have spent many days in seminars, spent a lot of money to find myself. Until I realized at some point that there was nothing to be found. I started meditating every morning and evening for four years. Then realized that I have done a lot but missed the most important thing—to recognize myself.

When I found myself, I became calm. I just sat there and recognized what was going on inside of me without wanting to achieve anything. Perhaps, for some people, this may seem completely normal, but most of us are out to "achieve" something in all areas of our lives. This may be good career wise, but, especially in personality work and in spirituality, this is counterproductive. At least that's my experience. So I sat there and listened to my inner self. First there were lots of thoughts and my patterns of wanting to do something. But at some point, it got quiet. That was the moment in which I felt, for the first time in my entirety, my "true greatness." That was the moment of the "I am!" Nothing else, just being.

Despite that moment of silence, I felt connected to everything. I felt the unity that is talked about so much. The nothing became everything at that moment. I realized that there was nothing else needed as the "I am." It's the greatest we can achieve by doing nothing.

It took me so many years to reach this moment. You can experience this much faster with the source consciousness.

EXPERIENCE THE LIGHTNESS AND POWER OF "I AM"

Find a comfortable place where you can be undisturbed for the next fifteen minutes. If possible, leave your eyes open. Make sure you are calm and relaxed. Then go into source consciousness. Find the gap between your thoughts. Expand the gap for as long as possible. If you still have a thought, try to ignore it, and remain in the "emptiness." Practice it until you manage to stay in source consciousness for fifteen minutes—although there is nothing to achieve.

That's it? Yes, it's that simple. It's not complicated; it's that easy. How did you feel during the exercise? What did you experience? Has your view changed? Were you able to enter the unity awareness? If not, then repeat the exercise ever so often. There will be the moment when you will be able to experience all of it.

EXPERIENCE YOURSELF IN SOURCE CONSCIOUSNESS

"The nothing is everything. Everything is nothing."

Repeat the "I am" exercise with the intention to experience yourself, your very own energy, your "true greatness," your strength and power. Speak your intention out loud once, and go again for fifteen minutes or longer into source consciousness. Be completely free of any expectations.

In source consciousness, the field in which everything is connected, anything is possible. To "just be" means to let go of everything. If it doesn't work, you may have unconscious expectations. Our ego is very tricky. I recommend doing the exercise with the kinesiological muscle test first. The body doesn't lie. Ask yourself the question, "Am I free from expectations?" And then do the test.

Remember: trying to "achieve" something with this exercise is counterproductive.

GRATITUDE

"Gratitude is, after love, the biggest force in the universe."

You can read everywhere how important it is to be thankful. Gratitude seems to have a power of its own. This is one of the teachings of quantum consciousness. My wife, Sonja, is an artist. For many years, she is painting "star gates" and published a wonderful book about it.[83] One of the star gates is the one of gratitude. The message of the painting is called, "Gratitude is a result of peace, a peace that lives within." Gratitude is a feeling. This feeling can fulfill you when you realize how much you have accomplished in your life. Gratitude flows through you when you are happy and when you accept the gift that life gave you. Be thankful for who and what you are and who you can be. Be thankful for being on earth and for the love that you can experience. Gratitude is part of happiness and blessings, a part that nourishes you and that offers you contentment. Be open to everything that's about to come. Be thankful for the here and now. Be thankful for your past, all of it. Be thankful for the gifts in the future that you will gratefully accept. Enjoy every moment and be thankful because every moment is important in your life. You are important. When gratitude is present, you will forget sorrow. Focus on the beautiful things that are present now. It will attract beautiful moments like a magnet. Open yourself up to gratitude for all the blessings that you bring and can experience. "It's a holy moment."

---

[83] Sonja von Staden, *Star Gates—Messages from the Light Sources* (Schirner Publisher, 2010).

The Stargate of Gratitude

It is often easy for us to be grateful for the good things. But especially for those moments that bring us anger and suffering, it is important to be grateful. In the end, this situation is just pointing out something. If we are aware of it, this situation is a great gift. I would like to give you an example:

In 2001, I started working as a project manager at a well-known bank. I had worked hard to get accepted for an interview with his bank, and the interview went so well. I really wanted to start there. I didn't get the job that I wanted, but in with the company. I really liked my new job, and, after four weeks, I even found myself in the area for which I originally applied for. Sometimes it just takes a little bit longer. Remember this quote from the second part? So I did a great job, had nice colleagues, etc. But the reality check came faster than expected. Within five months, during a conversation with my supervisor, I found out that I would not "survive" the probationary period. I could not believe it. They wanted to terminate me with my flawless work and résumé? My world collapsed.

It was at the time—at least it felt this way—I experienced the biggest tragedy of my life.

Today I am infinitely grateful that the termination took place. It was the starting point for my self-employment, which I started eighteen months later. Without this experience, I would certainly not have started my own company, and I would not have authored this book. I could give you many of these examples, and you may know many situations from your own life for which you are, in retrospect, thankful for. If we are honest, every situation has made us the person we are today. Even if our mind doesn't understand that every aspect of our life has a meaning, it is valuable to be grateful for these moments.

Even the law of attraction gets propelled when we manifest what we want in gratitude.

THE GRATITUDE RITUAL

Say thanks for everything right after you get up every morning and for what will or could happen during the day. Be thankful for your health, for your being, for your gifts, your success, etc., as everything is already a reality.

Before going to sleep, say thanks for all the situations and experiences you had during the day, for the big and small things, for the beautiful and for the not-so-perfect ones.

Finish the exercises also with a thank-you! It is a great helper to improve your life. That's worth a thank-you, isn't it?

ACTIVATE UNUSED SPIRITUAL POTENTIAL

"Why wander into the distance? See the good that is so close!"
—Johann Wolfgang von Goethe

I know many people that are on their spiritual path but have the feeling of being stuck somehow. This may have different reasons. There is still something to be learned before they can take another step forward, or there is a deep-seated pattern, behavior, or belief which prevents them from getting any further. It is important to explore what is blocking you. It is often the fear of our own power. A spiritual teacher once said,

"It's not being small that we're afraid of. It is our size that we shy away from."

I experience this over and over in my coaching and training sessions—understandable. When we accept all our strength and power that is within us, then we have a very great responsibility. Many people shy away from accepting it.

Find out what is holding you back. Get to know yourself better. Understand and see where and how you manipulate yourself. The following exercise can help you.

QUANTUM ENERGY AND SPIRITUALITY

EXPLORE OBSTACLES ON THE SPIRITUAL PATH

Find a partner you trust. Take enough time for this exercise and yourself. Get a notepad and pen ready. Make yourself comfortable, and sit in front of each other. Give the notepad to your counterpart so that they can write down what you will tell them.

Your counterpart is just sitting there and will listen to you during the exercise. Close your eyes. Go within yourself. Should you still have a lot of thoughts from everyday life buzzing around in your head, imagine how these thoughts are like clouds in the sky fading away by a powerful sun dissolving them to release a bright blue sky.

Visualize your spiritual path in whatever way you are perceiving it. Observe your path in details, what it looks like from now into the future. Do you see anything that slows you down? Is there a stone blocking your path? Speak it out loud. Take your time.

When you have looked at everything up close, go a little deeper. Feel within yourself, and pay attention to your body's reaction. How does your body react when you see your spiritual path further down? Is it tingling somewhere? Is your stomach pulling together? Does fear come up? Explore yourself deeper. Speak out loud what you feel. Speak about what is there right now. Feel and tell. No matter what comes up.

When nothing else comes up, open your eyes. Feel for a moment, and let your partner tell you what they just heard.

Have you been able to gain new knowledge about yourself? This can be considered a first aid. It is my experience that if we explore ourselves and listen carefully, a great deal of information can flow. For more in-depth information, a coach or other experts would be the right contact.

I presented an exercise to you that can be used to awaken the unused potential in relation to your greatest gift. The same exercise also enables you to uncover your unused spiritual potential. Perform the exercise as described—with the difference that you think at the beginning of the exercise about your spiritual potential. The sequence stays the same.

REALIZE YOUR OWN MASTERY

"The path of mastery begins and ends with you."

In my life, I have been able to experience one thing in particular: that life is a mastery. Every single day of my life, I experience, do, and understand more. This brings me a little further on my spiritual path. Every experience leads to a new understanding, assuming I pay attention to what the experience was good for. With each understanding, my consciousness expands, and I have the chance to change it to something positive in my life. The more conscious I get, the further I am on my path of mastery. And it probably doesn't end until I take my last breath. The process of becoming aware goes through four phases:

- Unconscious incompetence
- Conscious incompetence
- Conscious competence
- Unconscious competence

The first phase can easily be described as "functioning." For example, use an obstructive belief like "I have to be perfect." For some reason, you have experienced at some point that it is important to do everything perfectly. This belief is therefore part of your life and determines it significantly. You act accordingly but unconsciously. At a time, you are at a seminar for personality development and find out during an exercise that you have this belief and how much you have mastered this belief pattern. Now you are aware of your "chains," and you arrived in phase two. That's good, because now you have the opportunity to change something. Unless you do not want to change anything. Thanks to the life's model, you know that you can change only when changing your beliefs. New behavior alone is of no use. So you are coming home from the seminar, for example, remembering the book you are currently holding in your hands, seeking out the appropriate exercise to change your belief patterns. After the exercise, you will have a lot of new tools in front of you but still a tender little seed which needs to be properly cared for. This is phase three. The more you water the seed, the more it will grow and thrive. That is, the more you apply your new beliefs in everyday life—in other words, act accordingly—the stronger the "trunk" becomes. The "new" will become a routine. You are now in phase four.

This is the mastery of your life. The more you go into the phase of unconscious competence, the more clarity you will get. This will lead you to a life full of abundance, joy, and contentment.

EXPERIENCE THE ESSENCE

> "You were striving for enlightenment and had to find out later that you were already enlightened."

Our ego wants to own. That's why we speak about having peace, having wealth, etc. The ego is our structure. It serves only one purpose—to ensure our survival. Therefore, you need peace, love, etc. But in the moment of possession, we haven't internalized peace and wealth, much less internalized and really felt it. This is one of the reasons why many people that are rich are still fearful that they might lose it again. They are dissatisfied and unfulfilled and don't feel rich. It is the same with peace. A manager and the workman's comp council can make peace through an arbitrator, but both parties will observe carefully how the other acts because they feel no peace. Only when we can feel all of it inside ourselves can silence happen. Then real peace occurs. No storm can harm a person who is at rest. A person that feels love in their heart does not know jealousy and doesn't envy. You can let others be because you know that there is nothing to lose.

FEELING THE DIFFERENCE BETWEEN HAVING AND BEING

Perform the following test: Please say the sentence "I have peace," and feel what it does to you. What is happening in you? What kind of response does it trigger? Now speak the next sentence: "I am peace." How does that feel? Can you tell the difference? The "I am" also finds here its strength. The phrase "I have peace" cannot be felt.

Therefore, it is clearly weaker than "I am peace." In the moment of feeling, you recognize the value of the sentence.

Feeling truly deeply is a mastery. It is the wisdom of quantum consciousness. The power of the heart is up to five thousand times stronger than that of the mind; it is the knowledge of the new sciences.

The next exercise is to get to the bottom of the terms when we experience the essence. During the experience, you are in the being of "I am." The foundation of this exercise is to stay long within the source consciousness. On this level, the moment of absolute calm and emptiness, are you able to feel the essence:

- The essence of love
- The essence of peace
- The essence of freedom
- The essence of inner riches
- The essence of truthfulness
- The essence of compassion
- The essence of calm
- The essence of power

EXPERIENCE THE ESSENCE OF LOVE

Make yourself comfortable, and close your eyes. Be aware that this exercise will only work if you can be fully engaged in it, being free of expectations. Get calm and relax. Then go into the source consciousness. When you are fully engaged in it, think about the word "LOVE".

Let yourself be drawn into the word as if you would be pulled deep down into a water vortex. The deeper you dive, the more your approach the knowledge of the essence of love. At some point, you can't go any deeper. This point will find you. You will recognize it. Immediately! In this moment, you are penetrated into the essence of love. Linger there, and feel the essence completely. Just let it happen. Wait until your being has fully absorbed this essence. You will know when the time is right. Then let go and come back slowly to the here and now at your pace. Let go of the source consciousness, and open your eyes. Just feel yourself afterward. What happened?

This exercise is simple and, at the same time, infinitely valuable. Only a few people can reach this point. Just take it all in. Afterward you can go on with your everyday life. You don't have to name what just happened to you. Take your time so that the essence can settle in you and your consciousness can fully expand.

The Essence

Say the phrase "I am love!" again later. Feel and see what happens to you as a result that you have now experienced the essence of love. The sentence "I am love!" probably has a completely new value to you. Bring this value in your everyday life—and your life can change significantly.

EXPERIENCE THE UNIVERSAL IMPULSES

"There it was, a miracle, and it passed you by."

You probably have already asked yourself how you can receive the universal impulses and how you know they are the right ones. We get many of these impulses every day, but we rarely recognize them, or we are not focused on them.

Imagine you're in town out shopping, and, for some reason, you suddenly feel the urge you should go into this cell phone store. Your inner dialogue could be *What am I supposed to do in this shop? I already have a cell phone. There are no problems with my phone.* Or *What am I supposed to go in this shop for? I can still recall the argument with the telephone company from last year.* And so you go on and don't worry about it anymore. But what would have happened if you had followed this impulse? Perhaps you would have met your future partner in there. Maybe you would have an idea during the conversation with the associate that would bring you closer to your goals or your visions. This stop could also make you to hang out in the city a bit longer.

Because of that reason, you would avoid a traffic accident that would have occurred on the highway that you are now driving on later. They're all hypothetical possibilities you may think now. Maybe, maybe not. You know, there are no coincidences. These impulses are important pointers on your way. I learned to listen to them.

Universal impulse

What can you do to be more aware of these impulses and to develop them? I recommend the following exercise.

EXPANSION OF THE PERCEPTION FOR THE UNIVERSAL IMPULSES

Find a place where you can be undisturbed and comfortable. Sit or lie down. Close your eyes. Make sure that you are very comfortable. Then focus on your breath as it comes and goes. With every breath you take, you can relax a little more. Every breath will take you deeper. Go onto the path of silence.

Now prepare yourself for a journey, a journey to a wonderful place. This can be a place where you've already been or always wanted to go. Imagine how you're going there now, how and where and with whom you like to be there with. Arrive at this place now. First look around. Where are you exactly? What does that place look like? What do you feel? What do you see? Make yourself comfortable there. While you are making this space really cozy for you, you can see on the horizon far back a light that is getting bigger and bigger. It's getting closer. The closer it gets, the more it's taking on a shape. You recognize a silhouette that resembles a body but only consists of light. While you can't still make out what it is, you can feel how it becomes more comfortable the closer the light gets. Your heart is warm. You feel extremely comfortable and secure—full of love.

You know that what is getting closer is something good, something wonderful. After all, this light body, this light path, this luminous figure seems to radiate this immense love. The love that this being radiates is immersing through your entire body and shines all its love onto you until you are as full of light as this being. Your body is now full of light and love. Feel this heavenly moment. Now feel how this being is touching your third eye. This is the point two fingers wide and above the bridge of your nose. Through this touch, you can feel how something changes at once, becomes wider, and opens up. Whatever it is you feel, your perception expands and opens up to a new perspective. Feel what is happening, and immerse yourself in it, this new field of consciousness.

Thank the being of light for this gift while it's already retreating backward toward the horizon and disappearing, becoming smaller and smaller, until it has faded away. Linger a moment longer, and enjoy yourself at your place. Prepare yourself for your way back. Look back at your wonderful place, and return to the here and now. Feel how you are sitting or laying there. Feel the area under your body, feel your legs, your torso, your arms, and your head. Take the time to fully arrive in the here and now. Move your fingers and feet. Then open your eyes. Welcome back.

Now it is up to you to recognize these impulses that you will perceive more and more. Act on them.

EXPERIENCE THE SOUL AND BODY AS A UNIT

> "Don't try to distinguish between body and soul!
> The body is immersed in its soul like the soul in its body."
> —the Talmud

Often I meet people that tell me that they somehow feel strange in their own body.

They would not be quiet "here" and would feel uncomfortable. When asking them if they like to be on earth, they answered that they don't. They also like to "flee" into a dream world. Others feel energetically cut off at a certain point of their body. They really don't feel their body or just a part of it, and, although the nerves are perfectly fine, they often lack the grounding, the connection, with earth.

There may be different reasons for this. One could be that the soul is not properly connected to the body. Usually the soul enters the body completely at the moment of birth.[84] Due to complications at birth, such as Cesarean section or other childbirth complications, it can happen that only part of the soul moves in. Because of this, described feelings as mentioned above can occur. What options are there for these individuals to be more grounded? I can recommend the following:

---

[84] There are different statements in regard to the subject on patterns. Some say that the soul is entering the body at birth; others mention that this is already happening during conception. Ultimately, the timing is not relevant, but the result is that the soul is only partially in the body.

GROUND YOURSELF

Do this exercise while sitting or standing. When sitting down, place your feet next to each other. Close your eyes. Imagine roots growing out of your feet, which are getting longer and longer and deeper into the ground and become more like branches. Let these roots grow deeper and deeper into the center of the earth. Feel how you get more connected to Mother Earth, melt and grow together. Feel how you are firmly rooted. Feel the energy radiating from it that flows into your body. You are now a unit with Mother Earth. After a while, come back to the here and now, and open your eyes.

You can do this exercise often, especially whenever you feel that you are not quiet "here."

In order to find a permanent solution, a more complex exercise is required that you already know, which is "the transformation of the cell consciousness." With this exercise, you will be able to repeat the process of helping the soul to enter into the body completely, which did not happen previously or completely.

As mentioned in other parts, I also recommend recording the exercise either on your cell phone or have someone read it out slowly to you or use the CD "the Transformation of the Cell Consciousness" to firmly anchor the soul into the body.

The Soul moving into the body

TRANSFORMATION OF CELL CONSCIOUSNESS—ANCHORING THE SOUL FIRMLY INTO THE BODY

As always, do the kinesiological test first to see if it is now the appropriate time to perform this exercise.

Sit or lie down. Close your eyes. Place your hands on or next to your body. Pay attention to your breath as it comes and goes. Focus on your breathing. Then take three deep breaths. Feel how the oxygen fills your lungs, how your chest and stomach are raising and lowering. Just keep breathing in your own personal rhythm. Notice how your body relaxes more with each breath.

Now let your entire life go backward in your mind. This usually happens quickly, but take the time you need. Go back through your entire adulthood, back to your young adult hood, to adolescence, to your childhood, to early childhood, all the way back to birth. Notice your birth. Go through the period of growing up in your mother's womb, back to the time of your conception. Feel your procreation and then go back a little further. Now you are merely still a soul. Now stop. Enjoy the time as a soul in which you are completely free. Here is perfect, unconditional love. Here is all the knowledge of the universe, absolute peace and quiet, perfection in its purest form. You can feel all of it. The connection to all souls in the universe, the oneness with everything and with God.

Even if you would like to stay here forever, remember that you want to come back to earth—to gain experiences. So now decide for a new life, and feel how this decision generates new energy that will set a new pattern. Prepare for your life. Then it starts. Witness as the soul how your future parents make love, close together, and are just about to create a child: you! Watch the egg cell and sperm cell merge with each other, and you, as the soul, are part of this wonder. Notice how the first cells start to divide, then two cells become four, then eight, sixteen, etc. More and more cells are created, and, with each cell division, more life is created. Every single cell is flooded with love. See how you grow from embryo to fetus. Arms and legs as well as all organs develop. You grow in the womb and feel how the life force grows bigger and bigger. You are looking forward to seeing the light of day soon. Tune yourself into the vibration and energy of being a human.

Then it's time. You are about to be born. Prepare yourself to move as a soul into the body. It is exciting because, from now on, you can gain many experiences as a human. All is perfectly aligned. Many other souls are watching you in full anticipation because they all know about this miracle. Then comes the moment of birth. Feel how you melt at the moment of birth—as a soul and human being, just like the egg and the sperm cell at the time of procreation. Feel the miracle of how your soul becomes one as a human.

Whatever may happen during birth, slip completely into your body. Now celebrate that union of life, and scream out loud. Do it just in your thoughts or through your mouth. Scream out, and look forward to life.

Now everything is going very quickly. You are in your early childhood. Experience yourself in oneness with body, mind, and soul. Everything is so different, so new. Feel yourself as a unit, feel this wholeness. Feel your whole body connected to earth. And every moment that is now different than before changes your DNA structure. Your cell consciousness is transforming, and it's like all your cells are getting a new imprint. Your life changes, and so does your memory. You experience your childhood in a completely new way, although the situations are staying the same.

You grow up from child to adolescent, and you feel your body completely. You are looking forward to every day. Feel how your strength and confidence in life is getting stronger and stronger. You are grown up now and closer to the present. At some point, you have arrived in today.

But let life flow into your future. Feel how you are getting older and experience a wonderful future. You are enjoying your future to the fullest. You are loving life. Right before you arrive on the day your soul would leave your body, stop!

Look back to the present. What did you experience? What have you been doing all these years? How did you live? How did you experience your parents and your children?

How did the complete merging of body and soul change your life? Who was with you? What special situations have you experienced that influenced your life? What have you done about it? Take a close look at your timeline. See that the merging completely renewed your cell consciousness? Wonderful! Thank yourself for your life that you have created. You alone have created this miracle.

Now travel back to the present. Once arrived, feel your body. Recognize where you are sitting or lying. Focus on your breath as it comes and goes. Take three more deep breaths and come back to the today consciousness—into the here and now. Open your eyes when the time is right for you. Take your pen and notepad, and write down what you have experienced. The more detailed you describe everything, the more you will remember.

Welcome to your new life which is actually your old one. And yet a lot has just changed. Your soul was finally allowed to take its place after all these years, where it always belonged. Look forward to what will come—whatever it will be.

EXPERIENCE EVERYDAY LIFE COMPLETELY NEW WITH THE HELP OF SOURCE CONSCIOUSNESS

> "When everyday life becomes enlightenment, nothing will remain questionable."

Change your everyday life by letting the source consciousness incorporate more and more into your daily routine. Stretch the gap's sequence and widen it. You will experience a new way of seeing. The colors in which you perceive your surroundings become much stronger and become brighter, just like a Blu-ray or HD television in a whole new quality. All senses will become intensified; your perception and consciousness will expand and widen.

All of this can happen when you experience your everyday life in source consciousness. This can also be challenging while everyday life's tasks may distract you. You may have to practice daily, but it is absolutely worth practicing.

Welcome to life—to quantum consciousness. Welcome to the world that has always been meant to be for you. Enjoy it every day more and more.

QUANTUM ENERGY AND SPIRITUALITY

The world shines in a new light.

QUANTUM ENERGY AND DISTANT HEALING

> "Science states, that space and time are merely an illusion to understand life."

Before we get to the end of the book, I'd like to mention the aspect of distant healing. Quantum physics has, through its experiments, found out that space and time are only illusions. But we need this four-dimensional space of length, width, height, and time to orientate ourselves in our world. When we allow the knowledge of quantum physics to be integrated into our view of the world, miracles are possible that our mind can't even fathom.

In the latest experiments on the principle of entanglement, scientists were already able to beam the smallest quantum light particles, the photons. That means they teleported information from one place to another with the help of photons. Something similar was only known from *Star Trek* or other science fiction movies.

In the training to become a quantum energy coach, with the support of the wisdom of quantum consciousness, we are also getting support from distant dimensions. Does that sound too crazy to you? Have I lost my mind at the end of the book? I don't think so, because it is actually possible. Remember, if you expand your awareness and allow yourself to do things that your mind cannot understand, you too will perform miracles. Would you have believed twenty years ago that everyone will walk around with a little device against their ear, being able to talk to anyone in the whole world, calling it a cell phone? Or that one day you can hang your television on the wall?

That a three-inch stick called a USB would fit sixty-four thousand megabytes of storage space (the equivalent of around sixteen DVD-quality movies)? We are still ways away from our limits. Open up new dimensions for yourself.

Just as unusual and simple is distant healing. You can easily do this if you keep one important thing in mind: the person receiving the healing should know about the healing. It would be considered abuse of power when you simply heal someone without their knowledge. Maybe the person doesn't want to be healed at all. There may be a good reason why the person is sick or in pain. It is important to clarify this first before you would apply "quantum energy."

Secondly, it could be possible that this person is active at the moment, for example, riding a bike, etc. A distant healing, in this case for the driver and its direct environment, is extremely risky. If the person gives you consent to do the exercise, make an appointment for distance healing. Then the person can adjust accordingly. If the person can't agree to the exercise and something may hinder them, let them take the kinesiological test. Make sure it makes sense and would be the appropriate time to perform this exercise.

Distant healing is wonderful and has helped thousands of people. How does this work? Quite simply, like every exercise—with the difference that you only work with the other person in your imagination. There are different possibilities for the implementation:

1. You imagine the person in front of you and lead the corresponding exercise as you learned it through this book.
2. You imagine the person sitting or standing in an agreed place and then work with them as if you were standing close to them.
3. You can take a doll or a stuffed animal on which you perform the exercise on while thinking about the person that wants to be healed.
4. You perform the exercise on yourself while you are thinking about the other person.

The process in each case is the same.

CLOSING WORD

You have come to the end of my book. I thank you for making the decision to learn and to experience the wisdom of quantum consciousness. Reading alone won't change anything in your life, should you have read it only this far. Only practicing and applying the various exercises will turn your life into one exciting new adventure.

You may be familiar with some of these exercises. You can repeat and strengthen them. You may have asked yourself the question what one or the other exercise has to do with "quantum energy." It's like I described in the beginning.

"Quantum energy" is, in my essence, the most successful method and technique that I have gotten to know over the years. It serves only one purpose: to enable change and healing as soon as possible. You can then live the life that you want and what is your birthright—a life in abundance on all levels.

Perhaps you have noticed that you can use different exercises to address a specific topic. That's exactly how it should be. Because everybody is different. While one is achieving great results with "source consciousness," the other with "the transformation of cell consciousness." Meditations may work best for the next. Find out which exercises resonate best with you, because, ultimately, the final result counts. This is what "quantum energy" is all about: the variety of possibilities to achieve an optimal result.

If, for whatever reason, there is no change in you, make yourself aware of the "triangle" that "quantum energy" represents—understand, change, act. Maybe it's not your time yet. Perhaps you haven't understood yourself well enough and why these subjects are in your life, so the learning process would not be completed yet. Real understanding is the gateway to change and cure. That way everything comes into the flow. Make sure that the change and healing will take place so your life will change. Become active. Use your creative potential. Only then is the "triangle" complete.

Please feel free to contact me about what you have experienced during the exercises. If you have any suggestions or comments, don't hesitate to email me. I am looking forward to receiving any feedback at feedback@siranus.com

If you are also enthusiastic about the new learning of "quantum energy," I recommend referring the book to your friends, acquaintances, and colleagues. You are helping to ensure that more and more people are led to experience a fuller life on all levels.

Would you like to experience "quantum energy" in person? My pleasure. For more information and how you can get in touch with us, please see below. You will find plenty of information on our events, videos, and a "testimonial" report. You can experience my work live in different places around the world and soon throughout the United States:

- Quantum Energy Adventure Evenings
- Quantum Energy Coaching
- Quantum Energy Adventure Day
- Quantum Energy Adventure Weekend
- Quantum Energy Intensive Workshops on the Four Areas of Life
- Health/Relationships/Success, Job, Wealth, and Spirituality, as well as the explanation of one's own consciousness
- Training as a Quantum Energy Coach
- Specials in Ibiza

I am looking forward to getting to know you personally, and I wish you all a wonderful, happy, and fulfilling life.

With all my heart, best regards,
Siranus

Further information about Quantum Energy is available at www.QuantumEnergyCoaching.com, about the Author www.siranus.com, and you can reach our team under, support@quantumenergycoaching.com

TESTIMONIALS ON WORKING WITH "QUANTUM ENERGY"

Quantum energy, a part of my life

In November 2009, I took part in a "quantum energy" experience evening with Siranus Sven von Staden. That evening was overwhelming. Not only did I get more curious but I also wanted more. In February 2010, I started my training as a "quantum energy coach."

Since then, my life has undergone major changes. The person who I was a year ago does not exist in this form anymore. At first, I thought, *Great, I finally got a tool and a method that I can use to help many people with.* That I would help myself the most, I wasn't aware of first. That realization came later.

For me, the greatest importance of "quantum energy" is rooted in the healing or self-healing. Blockages I had to deal with half of my life and had not found any possibilities to recognize or change, I am now aware of and able to understand and could finally resolve. The process was gentle and initiated and directed me since then to my "true greatness."

"Quantum energy" has become a part of my life. I have recognized that I can make a choice every day: "How do I feel"? "What do I want in my life"?" and so on. I have learned to recognize blockages very quickly and to not let the momentum take over on its own. For me, "quantum energy" also means being able to change my point of view on different things. If I don't like something, well, then I change it. Knowing oneself through this method is like a revelation. Fears were allowed to go, and stepping into clarity and contentment followed.

So much has changed in my life in one year that it feels like a rebirth, like a second chance. My sensory perception has refined, and so has my physical sensation improved significantly. Pain was replaced with joy. My relationship with myself, as well as with my partner, child, family, friends, etc. has changed positively. A respectful and, above all, loving interaction is now possible.

Every day I experience "little miracles" that I create myself: the parking spot right in front of the store, an available concert ticket for the long "sold out" concert, and many more. The greatest gift I could do for myself is finally being able to change and to be myself. All you need is the willingness to do so. The insights that result from the development of possibilities should by no means be feared. It's the opposite: you are preparing for a new beginning.

Life is waiting to be finally lived. I am wishing you lots of fun with it!

—Anuschka Klinkhammer, Pulheim, Germany

PERCEPTION REDEFINED

"Quality of life", "my faith," and "the meaning of my life" are important topics to me. At the time, I asked myself how I can draw more of it into my life. What is good for me, what makes me happy, and how I can be and develop into the best version of myself—for the benefit of all!

There were always the questions: What is reality? Which energy determines and shapes our life? Is there anything at all? What is that what I feel as strength? And how can I use it?

After reading many books and viewing movies about these subjects, I was looking for a practical way to integrate all things easily and quickly into my everyday life. So I started my training as a "quantum energy coach" at the beginning of 2010 with Siranus Sven von Staden. My expectations were fulfilled. His knowledge that he has put together from various methods has a strong foundation. He relates his knowledge to us trainees with a lot of heart, joy, and talent. I found it amazing how quickly each of us has learned to implement this potential of healing on all levels.

One of my favorite methods is working with the source awareness. My clients feel comfortable with the exercise and feel a tingling sensation and energetic warmth flowing through them. For myself, within seconds, I feel a shiver during the exercise. I get goose bumps during this process of healing when healing begins. Not only my clients feel extremely comfortable but I also feel a deep sense of well-being, joy, and gratitude.

A lot has changed on my level of perception. I recognize very quickly what my subject is: "answer," "letting go," "distance yourself," or "serenity." I listen to my intuition and experience days later or someone tells me something that fits exactly to the subject. My awareness makes it much easier to develop myself and to find solutions to problems. It is also called "problem" and not "contra-blem." There is always a solution. We are sometimes a little "blind" to recognize them! "Quantum energy" helped me to be more attentive in this regard and to feel more solution oriented. If I have any questions about anything, I will use the relevant information, meditations, and exercises. I will receive an answer for myself within a short time. I can help myself and others to experience and have a better quality of life on all levels. For the best of all of us.

—Ariane Kolkmann-Rumpf, Bothel,
www.a-und-o-marketing.de

TESTIMONIALS

CLOSING WORDS (WITH GRATITUDE)

At this point, I would like to thank all of those who, in their own way, contributed to this book.

First of all, I would like to thank my wife, Sonja. Without her I would never have come across this wonderful publisher. It was her who handed my manuscript over and introduced me to the publisher Markus Schirner, Germany. The loving growth of our relationship has contributed to the part "Quantum Energy and Relationships." Sonja was also available for many practical exercises. Thank you for your great love and support.

I would like to thank my ex-wife, Anita, without whom I would never have met Sonja. It was her who gave and showed me a completely new feel of life despite any conformity.

A huge thank-you goes to my mother, Heide-Marie, and my deceased father Rüdiger. Without them I wouldn't be here today. Without them I would never have made and gathered all the experiences that led me to the person that I am today.

To my brother Frank, the one that had nothing to do with all of this transformation and healing work and then got deeply involved into the subject. He read with his correction glasses on and had suggested valuable changes.

I don't want to forget my wonderful fellow author Thorsten Weiss, who allowed me without hesitation to use his "physio magic" and to be included in this book.

My dear friend Sanja Viktoria Hamel who was the first to read the parts and made suggestions for improvement. Thanks for the constructive criticism as well as some new perspectives.

I would like to thank all my teachers who contributed to this book in their own way.

Thanks to all my coaching clients, seminar participants, and trainees through whom I learned to see how valuable and successful the work with "quantum energy" is. Thanks for the incredible amount of experiences that I could gather through them. I would like to point out all of those who have provided testimonials for the readers: through you, this book became even more practical.

Ultimately, thanks to all of the unnamed people who worked behind the scenes.

Without my dear friend and agent Rita LaRue, the book would never have come to life in the English version. Her vision was to bring *Quantum Energy* to the USA, where she resides for the past twenty-nine years, and ultimately into every English-speaking country. She, as a native German, translated the book and as my literature agent found Page Publisher. Thanks a million, Rita.

Shortly after the book became a bestseller in Germany and was translated into Dutch, French, Spanish and Polish, now we can reach many individuals with the English version. I would like to thank Page Publishing for their suggestions, cover-design ideas, and input. I would also like to thank my publication coordinator David Rodax for his support throughout the entire publishing process.

DIRECTORY

The Quantum Energy Method
Making "Miracles" Tangible
Experiencing Source Consciousness
Feel Source Consciousness
Contact

Quantum Energy and Health
Experiencing Source Consciousness Through Breath
Hindering Mental Beliefs / Statements of Beliefs
Changing Beliefs
Transformation of Cell Consciousness
Free Yourself of Fears
Activation Self-Healing Powers
Get Calm through Breathing
Stress Relief /Bathing in Source Consciousness
Feng Shui for the Brain
Assisting When Using Quantum Consciousness
The Restroom Meditation
Healing through Source Consciousness
Reactivate the Neurological Networks

Quantum Energy and Relationships
What Did I Learn About Love?
Self-Exploration: How Do I Feel the Lack of Love?
Healing Your Inner Child
Healing Love with the Support of Source Consciousness
The Love Diary

Transformation of Cell Consciousness—Finally Feeling Love Again
Stop, Challenge, Choose
Accepting One's Own Negative Patterns with Love
Ten Minutes for an Honest Relationship
Recognizing the Aspects of Your Parents within Yourself
The Parent Process
The Forgiveness Ritual
Reflecting on the Response to Your Child
In Touch with the Heart
Letting Go of Relationships

Quantum Energy and Success/Wealth
Feng Shui for the Brain 2
Seven Days That Will Change Your Life
The Dream Machine
What Do I Really Want?
The Vision Board
My Big Threes
Achieving Goals Easily
The Magical Power of Your Goal
Uncovering One's Own Untapped Potential
The Clear Direction
Transforming Blockages through One's Own Creative Power
Exchange the Belief in the Matrix
Clearing the Flow of Money
Increase the Flow of Money

Quantum Energy and Spirituality
Awakening Untapped Potentials to Strengthen Your Gift
Experienced the Lightness and Power of "I Am"
Experiencing Oneself in Source Consciousness
The Gratitude Ritual
Exploring Obstacles on the Spiritual Path
Feeling the Difference between Having and Being
Experiencing the Essence of Love

DIRECTORY

Expending the Perception for the Universal Impulses
Ground Yourself
Transformation of Cell Consciousness
Anchoring the Soul Firmly into the Body
Extended Literature
Bartlett, R. *Matrix Energetics* (VAK, 2010)
Bartlett, R. *Physics of Miracles* (VAK, 2010)
Bauer, J. *Why I Feel What You Feel* (Heyne, 2006)
Braden, G. *In Harmony with the Divine Matrix* (Koha, 2007)
Byrne, R. *The Secret* (Goldmann, 2007)
Canfield, J. *Compass for the Soul* (Goldmann, 2005)
Chopra, D. *The 7 Spiritual Laws of Success* (Ullstein TB, 2004)
Deida, D. *The Way of the True Man* (Kamphausen, 2006)
Deida, D. *You Are Love* (Kamphausen, 2008)
Eker, T. H. *This Is How Millionaires Think* (Heyne, 2010)
Ford, D. *The Dark Side of the Light Chasers* (Goldmann, 1999)
Ford, D. *The Shadow-Effect* (Kamphausen, 2011)
Fromm, E. *To Have or to Be* (DTV, 2005)
Grabhorn, L. *Wake up, Your Life Is Waiting* (Goldmann, 2004)
Kinslow, F. *Quantum Healing* (VAK, 2010)
Kinslow, F. *Experiencing Quantum Healing* (VAK, 2010)
König, M. *The Urwort* (Scorpio, 2010)
König, M. *Burnout* (Scorpio, 2012)
Krattinger, F. *Power Words* (Silberschnur, 2008)
Lipton, B. *Smart Cells* (Koha, 2006)
Lipton, B. *Spontaneous Evolution* (Koha, 2009)
McTaggart, L. *The Zero Point Field* (Goldmann, 2007)
Moritz, A. *The Liver and Gallbladder Miracle Cleanse* (Vox, 2011)
Nidiaye, S. *Learning to Feel Again* (Integral, 2006)
Pearl, E. *Reconnective Healing* (Koha, 2007)
Sheldrake, R. *The Creative Universe* (Ullstein, 2009)
St. John, N. *Success Is No Accident* (Ariston, 2010)
Takahashi, R. *Healing with Quantum Energy* (Books on Demand, 2009)

von Staden, S. *30 Minutes for the Confident Handling of Changes* (Gabal, 2010)
von Staden, S. *If Quantum Healing Doesn't Work* (Schirner, 2011)
von Staden, S. *Everyone Can Do Quantum Healing—Including You!* (Schirner, 2011)
von Staden, S. *Finally Bring Light into the Darkness of Your Beliefs*, Schirner 2012
von Staden, S. & von Staden, S *Ask Yourself Happy* (Schirner, 2012)
Weiss, T. *Spiritual Money Consciousness* (Schirner 2012)
Winget, L. *Shut Up, Stop Crying and Finally Live* (Heyne, 2009)
Williams, R. *Psych-K* (Koha, 2009)
Zurhorst, E. M. *Love Yourself and It Doesn't Matter Who You Marry* (Goldmann, 2007)
Zurhorst, E. M. and Zurhorst, W. *Love Yourself and Look Forward to It Next Crisis* (Goldmann, 2007)

DVD Recommendations
Awake, Allegria 2012
Bleep—Down the Rabbit Hole, Horizon 2007
Braden, G. In Harmony with the Divine Matrix, Koha 2009
The Movie of Your Life, Allegria 2011
The Gift—Why We Are Here, Scorpio 2010
Ford, D. The Shadow-Effect, Goldmann 2010
Goswami, A. The Quantum Activist, Horizon 2010
Lipton, B. Smart cells, Koha 2008
Lipton, B. How We Become What We Are, Koha 2009
The Living Matrix, Koha 2009
The Secret, Goldmann 2007
What the Bleep do we (K)now? Horizon 2006

Exercise CD Recommendations
Kinslow, F., Quantum Healing, CD 1 and 2, Koha 2010
Schirner 2013
S. von Staden, S. The Transformation of Cell Consciousness, Part 1–5, Schirner 2011/2012

DIRECTORY

von Staden, S. From Lack Awareness to Abundance Awareness, Schirner 2011

S. von Staden, S. Finally Free, Schirner 2011

S. von Staden, S. Non-Smoker in 8 Minutes, Schirner 2011

S. von Staden, S. So that Quantum Healing Has a Lasting Effect, Schirner 2011

S. von Staden, S. Finally Free From Limiting Beliefs, Schirner 2012

Weiss, T. Heal your Eyes, Schirner 2011

Weiss, T. Heal your Ears, Schirner 2012

ABOUT THE AUTHOR

Siranus Sven von Staden is an angel investor, business mentor, and master coach with a strong focus on entrepreneurial and female executives. Siranus supports every individual in their personal or business growth so intensively that nothing in life can limit them anymore.

After twenty years of experience with thousands of clients, he quickly recognizes the core and reason for their challenges. Through his power and intuition, he recognizes the smallest nuances, guides his clients with deep empathy, and laser-sharp clarity to a level that they have not known even exists, personally and in business.

No matter what issue everyone is facing in the beginning and how bad and intense it is, he will assist and guide each individual through the entire process of healing with one result in mind: boundless freedom and deep fulfillment on all levels!

Siranus is the founder of the worldwide applied transformation and healing method *Quantum Energy*. He is a two-time bestselling author in Europe with currently twenty-five books and audio books available in seven languages. He has appeared in well-known TV shows and magazines in Europe. He is also featured in the renowned German female of excellence magazine called *Erfolg Magazin*. Siranus lives now and works hybrid in Costa Blanca, Spain.